MATHEW CAREY

MATHEW CAREY

EDITOR, AUTHOR AND PUBLISHER

A STUDY IN AMERICAN LITERARY DEVELOPMENT

BY
EARL L. BRADSHER, Ph.D.

AMS PRESS, INC.
NEW YORK
1966

PREFACE

Mathew Carey, the subject of this study, after a lapse of three quarters of a century, has survived in chronological outlines and literary histories as the author of a *History of the Yellow Fever, The Olive Branch,* and of numerous works on political economy and a bewildering variety of subjects that defy classification.[1] As such he is not unworthy of study by the close student of American literature and history; but were he noteworthy as an author alone, an essay, rather than a monograph, would probably be his due. Carey's real claim to consideration is as a publisher, and, to a lesser extent, editor, and author. Our young civilization of a century ago, whether within the sound of the Atlantic or on that shifting belt known vaguely as the frontier needed a medium thru which literature could reach it in order that it might outgrow its provincialness and painful self consciousness. America itself was largely adequate, under proper stimulus, to produce a literature; and any omission could easily be filled from the mature literatures of Europe. Such a medium and such a stimulus Mathew Carey, better than any one else in this country, supplied for over half a century. At this formative period he was able to direct the taste of his public in a way not in the slightest degree possible for the publisher of today when the multiplicity of publishing houses, of authors, and of already developed tastes defies any attempt at control. From 1785 to 1817 Carey was the sole owner, and from 1817 to 1824 he was actively at the head of the greatest publishing and distributing firm in this country,[2]

[1] The titles of his books, pamphlets, and speeches occupy four pages of notes and seven of text in the *Bibliotheca Americana.*

[2] The titles of the various firms of which he was the founder or forerunner were as follows: Mathew Carey, 1787–1817; M. Carey & Son, 1817–1821; M. Carey & Sons, 1821–1824; Carey & Lea 1824. Subsequently Edward L. Carey, a son of Mathew Carey, was admitted. The business was divided in 1829 when Henry C. Carey and Isaac Lea (afterward Carey, Lea & Blanchard, and then Lea & Blanchard) formed a firm as publishers

and tho his formal connection with the house ended in the latter year there is no doubt that thru his sons he was influential, in its conduct until a much later period. Fortunately all the documents relating to his business from 1787 to 1823 are preserved, and they form one of the most interesting and valuable sources of information on the publishing business in America. Since it is very largely upon these documents that the present study is based the question naturally arises, How far can the business of these firms be regarded as typical of that of the entire country and how far do their publications and their sales of the books of other publishers represent the tastes of the reading public as a whole and not merely those of a section or class? The reasons for believing it to be typical, and therefore of value in enabling one accurately to trace the development of literary culture in America are numerous. It represents all phases of the business of the largest firm in Philadelphia, the acknowledged literary center of America during most of the period covered by this study. There was little or no specialization of publication as yet; so that when we examine the publications of Carey (and of his successors) we may be fairly sure that no other publisher is issuing a radically different class of books. We feel that this must be

exclusively, continued to the present day as Lea & Febriger, two members of the firm being Mathew Carey's great-grandchildren. When the firm was divided Edward L. Carey and Abram Hart formed the firm of Carey & Hart. With them we are not concerned. The account books begin January 1, 1787; the correspondence received, 1788. The correspondence sent out is very irregularly kept, or, an assumption that is probably more just to the various firms, has subsequently been misplaced. By a careful estimate the number of volumes is 510. Of this number 145 volumes, quarto, are letters received, forty are copies of those sent out. The remaining 325 volumes are made up of account books, day books, journals, receipt books, stock books, warehouse books, exchange lists, subscription lists, memorandum books, bills of lading, and all other material necessary to a complete business record. Between 1823 and 1854 there is a gap in the record. By chance, however, three volumes of letters sent out have survived covering the two periods of June 17, 1834 to August 6, 1837, and January 2, 1841, to June 10, 1842. After 1854, the firm, then known as Lea & Blanchard, published medical books almost exclusively.

the correct conclusion when we examine the exchange lists and notices of forthcoming publications which were sent out by various firms. The general class is always the same, and even the titles have a striking uniformity. The general nature and purpose of other firms was, then, very similar. As there is no great number of inquiries for books not kept on hand, it it a logical inference that the scope of the reading of the entire country fell fairly well within the limits of the literature disseminated by the firm in question, for the wide distribution of its business— from Castine, Maine, in the north to St. Louis and New Orleans on the west and south—indicates that the general demands of the country could be supplied. In any case the business must be typical of a large part of the south, for the firm was so well established there that it had no formidable competitor. The intense rivalry of a later period for the works of British authors shows that a large number of publishers were on the lookout for similar works.

The subject of this monograph was suggested by Professor W. P. Trent of Columbia University, under whom it was my privilege to study for almost three years. I, least of all, should be inclined to underestimate the breadth and the catholicity of judgment that so strikingly characterize the scholarship of Professor Trent and that are so abidingly felt by every student who has come under his influence, but it is above all as a personal friend that I wish here to express my gratitude to him.

I feel also that I am deeply indebted to Mr. Charles M. Lea, of Lea and Febiger, Publishers, Philadelphia. Mr. Lea has in charge the documents without which this study could not have been brought to completion. He has met, with a cheerful courtesy which it is a pleasure to acknowledge, every desire of mine regarding the material at his disposal. To his father, the late Henry C. Lea, whose name is known to every student of history, I am under obligations for having read the manuscript and having made several valuable additions. It is in this same connection that one of my most direct obligations to Professor Trent is due. There are few pages that have not been bettered by his suggestions. The manuscript has been read, also, by Professor Brander Matthews and Professor A. H. Thorndike of Columbia University, and by Professor C. N. Greenough of Harvard University, to all of whom I am under obligations for suggestions. Mr. Henry Carey Baird of Philadelphia and Mr. Albert Matthews of Boston have given me pamphlets of value bearing upon the subject.

CONTENTS

MATHEW CAREY

CHAPTER I

The First Steps: Journalist and Editor

Mathew Carey was born in Dublin, January 28, 1760,[1] of well-to-do parents. His education was that of the average boy of his time and circumstances. Unlike most boys however he had very early decided upon the trade which he wished to follow. At the age of fifteen he was apprenticed to a bookseller. This was accomplished thru his own efforts; for his father, while offering him the choice of any other of the twenty-five corporations in Dublin, refused to aid him in his resolution to become a printer and bookseller. In this position he had ample chance to satisfy his omnivorous appetite for reading, and the desire, not less strong, it seems, to rush into print. His first essay as a writer, at about the age of seventeen, was a severe condemnation of duelling, in a newspaper article in the *Hibernian Journal* in 1777. Years after in America he was to give a "practical illustration of the text."

[1] The published accounts of the life of Carey are very few in number. Those given below are all that I have been able to find.

American Bookseller, The, Vol. XVII, No. 3, New York, Feb. 1, 1885. Editorial Contributions to the Trade History—Number One. The Carey-Baird Centenary, January 25, 1885. Memoir of Mathew Carey, Founder of the House, by Henry Carey Baird, with a reproduction of " Carey's Pennsylvania Evening Herald " and Portrait of M. Carey, pp. 59–64.

Autobiographical Sketches, in a Series of Letters Addressed to a Friend, Philadelphia, 1829. 12mo, pp. xvi + 156. This was afterwards republished in *The New England Magazine* (July, 1833, to December 1834, the installments beginning as follows: V, p. 404, 489; VI, 60, 93, 227, 306, 400; VII, 61, 145, 239, 320, 401, 481).

Historical Sketches of Some of the Pioneer Catholics of Philadelphia and Vicinity, by Joseph Willcox (a pamphlet without date or place of publication containing 51 pages of text and 10 of plates at the end), pp. 17–20.

That intense love of country and of humanity, which was to win him the affection and respect of so many thousands in his adopted country, was very early shown in a pamphlet written in 1779[2] in defense of his oppressed fellow Irish Catholics. Self interest and a propitiatory attitude towards officialdom were never at any time strong features of his character. Very naturally, then, in dealing with so delicate a subject as " The urgent necessity of an immediate repeal of the whole Penal Code against the Roman Catholics," the ardent youth raised such a storm in governmental circles that his cooler headed friends thought best to ship him off to Passy, a village near Paris. Here the one extreme of character met the other: unhesitating impulsiveness and shrewd worldly knowledge came into contact, when Carey was engaged by Benjamin Franklin to reprint his dispatches from America. After a few months Franklin no longer had need for him, and he went to work with Didot *le jeune,* the greatest printer of his time, from whom he must have learned much about the technical part of his profession. There is little evidence that Franklin had any marked influence upon Carey. The dissimilarity of character and the difference in age were probably too great. Nor does their acquaintance later in America appear to have been other than of the most formal kind. One friendship of very great value later he did make—that of La Fayette.[3]

Once more in Dublin, where the storm had blown over, he proceeded to get into fresh trouble. In October, 1783, his father aided him to establish the *Volunteer's Journal.* In this he boldly defended the manufactures, commerce, and political rights of Ireland against the encroachments of Great Britain. The career of the *Journal* he described in after years

[2] *The urgent necessity of an immediate repeal of the whole Penal Code against the Roman Catholics candidly considered, to which is added an inquiry into the prejudices entertained against them; being an appeal to the Roman Catholics of Ireland, exciting them to a just sense of their civil and religious rights, as citizens of a free nation.*

[3] While Carey was an exile at Passy an invasion of Ireland was contemplated by the French, and La Fayette called upon him to make inquiries concerning the political condition of the country. Carey was unable however to give him any information of value.

as "enthusiastic and violent." As "enthusiastic," it excited the approbation of the Irish; as "violent," the disapprobation of the English. Carey was finally imprisoned for an article in which the Parliament in general and the premier in particular were denounced for their Irish policy. After living "joyously" in Newgate for a month he was released; but dreading the outcome of a suit for libel instituted in behalf of the premier, his friends persuaded him to emigrate to America, September 7, 1784.

For a while he hesitated between New York, Baltimore, and Philadelphia. He chose the last named because his case seemed better known there, and he concluded that the oppression he had undergone would gain him friends. There he was to remain until his death in 1839. As he had only a dozen guineas, and was unknown and friendless, the future did not look particularly promising. By chance a fellow passenger visiting Washington and Lafayette at Mount Vernon mentioned Carey's name and situation to the latter. When La Fayette arrived a few days later at Philadelphia, he requested Carey to call on him. They parted after half an hour's conversation, during which La Fayette promised to recommend him to Robert Morris, Thomas Fitzsimmons[4] and others. Nothing whatever was said about financial assistance. Judge then of Carey's surprise upon receiving, by letter the next morning, four hundred dollars from La Fayette, who had already departed for Princeton—a sum which Carey had the pleasure of returning to the donor on his next visit to America in 1824.

Thru this gift Carey was enabled immediately to establish the *Pennsylvania Herald*, January 25, 1785. The venture met

---

[4] Thomas Fitzsimmons (1741–1811) a victim of England's oppression of the Irish, came to America, probably in 1765, and settled in Philadelphia. He was an ardent supporter of the Revolution, and in 1780 his firm gave £5000 to aid the cause. He also raised and commanded a company of militia, and served at the battles of Trenton and Princeton. In 1782 he was a member of the Continental Congress, and, in 1787, a delegate in the framing of the Constitution. He was a representative to the first Congress, a strong advocate of a protective tariff up to 1795, and an opponent of universal suffrage.

with scant success until, on August 27, 1785, a regular series
of the debates of the House of Assembly was begun in its
columns. This was a new departure in American journalism,
and greatly increased the popularity of the paper. The inevitable political alignment soon took place; and Carey, Anti-
Federalist, in a short while found himself engaged in a bitter
controversy with the leader of the Federalists, Colonel Eleazer
Oswald. Not content with the opportunities afforded by his
newspaper, Carey published *The Plagi Scurriliad, a Hudibrastic Poem, addressed to Col. Oswald.* The Colonel's retort
was a challenge. In the duel that followed, Carey, lame since
early childhood, received just above the knee a wound that
was not healed for fifteen or sixteen months.

During this period the *Pennsylvania Herald* seems to have
been discontinued, so that Carey was free to start another
venture. In October, 1786, he began the *Columbian Magazine.* Evidently this was expected to be a very lucrative publication for there were five partners; but by the end of the year
Carey had withdrawn. In January, 1787, he issued the first
number of the *American Museum.* With this date begins his
real influence and importance in American literature.

The magazine, at least in America, was yet in its experi-
mental stage. Benjamin Franklin and Andrew Bradford in
1741 had issued the first monthly—*The General Magazine
and Historical Chronicle of all the British Plantations in America,*[6] but there had not been enough pioneers in the field to
clear the road for the newcomers. Warned by the ill fortune
of all his other ventures, it was not without considerable mis-
givings that Carey attempted a new one. He seems to have
turned to Jeremy Belknap, already well known as a literary
man and one well qualified to give advice on literary projects.
Belknap's reply, written from Boston, February 2, 1787, was,
in part, as follows:

" . . . Several attempts have been made within my memory
both here & at the Southward to *establish* such a repository of
Literature, but after a year or two they have uniformly failed.

[6] A. H. Smyth, *The Philadelphia Magazines and Their Contributors,*
Philadelphia, 1892, p, 22.

To what other Causes this failure may be ascribed I will not say—but this appears to me to be one, viz., the *too frequent* publication of them. We are fond of imitating our European Brethren (I speak of scientific Brethren) in their *monthly* productions—without considering the difference between our Circumstances & theirs. A Country full of learned men, full of business, literary, political, mercantile—having inexhaustible Resources of knowledge of every kind—may be able to keep up one or two monthly vehicles of Information so as to make a respectable appearance but such a Country as this is not yet arrived at such a pass of Improvement. Modesty is best in all new attempts & it is certainly the wisest way to begin as we expect to out. For these reasons were I to have the direction of a Magazine I would propose to publish it *Quarterly* & to increase its size as material should occur. I should also conduct it partly on the plan of the annual Register so as to establish a Connected history of Events, taking Care to keep far enough behind so that any Series or Period should lapse in point of action before the Relation of it begin. . . . "

To these admonitions Carey seems to have paid considerable attention, but he found that Belknap had underestimated the quantity of material at hand.

The first article, *Consolations for America,* by Benjamin Franklin, is indicative of the tone of the new publication. Hitherto all the magazines published in this country had looked across the ocean for their models. The American Revolution had nearly paralyzed the publishing business, and magazines published before that time were, almost without exception, intensely loyal in their attitude. Bradford, always complaisant to British suggestions and influences, had, in his *American Magazine,* strongly supported the crown against the French. Paine and Brackenridge had too often made their magazines merely a medium of attack upon the Tories. The *Columbia Magazine* had steered clear of all political problems, but had given much of its space to manufactures and agriculture. Now with the *American Museum* a complete American magazine begins. While avoiding any offensive partisan attitude, it nevertheless reflects the unsettled state of the country in those critical years before the adoption of the Constitution. Its articles are of so varied a nature that it presents the nearest approximation yet obtained to what our forefathers conceived

a magazine should be—a treasury of all human knowledge.
Tho to the *Columbian Magazine,* in its issue of August,
1789, fell the honor of introducing America's greatest novelist
before Cooper—Charles Brockden Brown[7]—the service of
Carey in giving the literary talent of our country a medium of
expression may be best judged by the number of familiar
names found in the *Museum.* The second article, in which
we get a glimpse of the politically unorganized condition of the
country—*Patriots and Heroes—the Revolution Is Not Over*
—is by Dr. Benjamin Rush. Paine's *Common Sense* is reprinted. Philip Freneau, Trumbull, and Col. David Humphreys are the most voluminous contributors of poetry, which
forms, on an average, one-fifth of each number. Trumbull's
M' Fingal is printed in full, as is also Col. Humphreys' *Poem
on the Happiness of America,* while to Francis Hopkinson,
whose name occurs repeatedly as contributor of both prose
and poetry in the lighter vein, is due the credit of starting, thru
his *Dialogue III* of *Dialogues of the Dead,*[8] the " muck rake "
in American literature, or to be more liberal, the somnolent
street-sweeping brigade of Philadelphia. Anthony Benezet
utters a protest against slavery, and Governor Livingston
and others use the *Museum* as their regular organ. It is true
that not all of the articles signed by these men occur here for
the first time, but the majority do; and the minority gain an
enlarged circle of readers. As meager as was our literary output at this period, it must have been much more so but for
such a medium of expression. To that comparative meager-
ness Carey attests when he says the opinion had been entertained that material enough to run a magazine was not obtainable; but he adds that, contrary to that expectation, material
beyond his needs rapidly accumulated. This was not strange,
considering his ideas of what a magazine should be: for tho
he always gave the preference to American writers and articles
he felt at liberty to draw from any source, published or unpub-
lished, on practically any subject.

[7] Brown's *Rhapsodist.* A. H. Smyth, *Philadelphia Magazines and their
Contributors,* Philadelphia, 1892, p. 153.
[8] Vol. I, pp. 223–6.

The historical spirit was always strong in Carey: we find him, in the preface to the number for January, 1788 (Vol. III), lamenting the loss to posterity of letters of commanders, accounts of battles, authentic state papers, and similar material, published during the Revolution, of which he had unique copies. In order to prevent the obscurity of some of the important events of the Revolution, he determines to publish as many as possible of these documents in the *Museum,* which is in fact a veritable mine to the historian of the period. Noah Webster also seems to have had the same idea of the historical value of a magazine, for on September 3, 1788, we find him, besides asking that Carey publish his *Progress of Dulness* in the *Museum,* suggesting that Winthrop's *Journal* should be added. About a month before, Timothy Dwight had sent " a very sensible Dissertation on the language of the Muhhekaneen Indians by Dr. Edwards of New Haven. I think it well suited to your design, fraught with valuable instruction to the world. Let me advise you to engage the assistance of that gentleman, as I know of none more learned & able in this country." Truly if the reader of that day found Hopkinson and a few —a very few—others too frivolous, he had but to turn the page.

As yet there was no idea of "art for art's sake" and Washington expresses but the common view of his time when he writes to Carey: "I will venture to pronounce, as my sentiment, that a more useful literary plan has never been undertaken in America, or one more deserving of public encouragement. . . . For my part, I entertain an high idea of the utility of periodical publications; insomuch that I could heartily desire copies of the Museum and Magazines, as well as common Gazettes, might be spread through every city, town, and village in America. I consider such easy vehicles of knowledge, more happily calculated than any other, to preserve the liberty, stimulate the industry, and meliorate the morals of an enlightened and free people."[9] There was as yet extremely little

---

[9] This letter and the letter to Poe, on pages 112–113, are the only letters quoted in this study which, so far as I know, have been previously published. This will be found in the Preface to *The Museum.* John Dickinson,

call for mere amusement: the masses needed and were clamoring for education. Life was too stern and practical for much else. One correspondent, a little later, enters a vigorous protest against the loss of space in an illustrated spelling book; besides, he writes, his pupils wear out the pages by turning them over to look at the pictures. The limited number of books and the comparative narrowness of scholarship created a public of deliberate readers, and the ability, necessary to the modern scholar, of skimming thru many books was unknown and unneeded.

At the beginning of Volume 3, January to June, 1788, Carey prints a list of his subscribers by states and countries, which shows the widespread habit of reading even at that period. With the exception of Vermont and New Hampshire all the states and territories of that time are represented. Considering the struggle for material existence and the slowness and uncertainty of transportation facilities this is a good showing. The Boston magazines probably account for the absence of subscribers in Vermont and New Hampshire. All the European countries prominent at that time, with the exception of Spain, are represented, and an unusual number of the West Indian Islands. The *Museum* well deserved the name of "the first really successful magazine in America." Yet the life of the editor was never above penury. At no time, according to his own statement, was he possessed of more than four hundred dollars.[10] The subscription of two dollars and forty cents a

William Livingston, Edmond Randolph, Ezra Stiles, Timothy Dwight, Francis Hopkinson, and many others sent letters or resolutions (published in the Preface) strongly approving of the project.

[10] This condition arose also from the fact that more than half of the subscribers lived in remote situations, often five hundred miles away, and remittances were slow. It was frequently necessary to dun these subscribers, thru hired collectors, at a heavy expense. Carey printed more copies than he had any immediate sale for in the vain hope that the subscription list would be ultimately enlarged. When he became a publisher of general literature he, in spite of the warnings of the *Museum*, continued for several years to publish and handle a stock about twice as large as his trade justified. It was necessary to borrow money heavily, and "I was shaved so close by the latter class (the usurers) that they almost skinned me alive. I have owed for months together from three to six

year was entirely too low for the thousand or eleven hundred pages furnished; remote subscribers refused to remit promptly; and too many copies were printed in expectation of a larger subscription. In December, 1792, the last numbers of the *Museum* and of the *Columbian Magazine* were issued. Both editors assign the same reason: "The present law respecting the establishment of the post-office, which totally prohibits the circulation of monthly publications through that channel on any other terms than that of paying the highest postage on private letters or packages."[11] Carey mentions as an additional cause the extension of his business as a bookseller, which renders him unable to give the *Museum* proper attention. Only once more was he to introduce a periodical to the public—*The Thespian Monitor and Dramatic Critic*, by Barnaby Bangbar, Esq., (1809)—a publication which did not live long.

The year after the suspension of the *Museum* a yellow fever plague swept over Philadelphia, and for a summer all industry was paralyzed. The readers of *Arthur Mervyn* will recall the vivid pages in which Brown describes the suffering of this summer. With more fidelity to fact[12] Carey has given us a complete

thousand dollars, borrowed from day to day, and sometimes in the morning to be paid at one o'clock the same day, to meet checks issued the preceding day. The horrors of this situation can scarcely be conceived by any person not experiencing them. I have worked, lame as I was, from nine or ten o'clock in the morning, till two or half past two, trying to borrow money." Yet "during this whole period, I scarcely ever disappointed a lender." (*Autobiography* in the *New England Magazine*, Vol. VI, pp. 227–8.)

It might be added in this connection that Carey's reason for writing the *Autobiography* was a desire to encourage those struggling under such difficulties as he had met, and to warn them against bad business methods. The motto of his sunny yet indomitable nature was, apparenly, Never Despair.

[11] Benjamin Franklin, in his *Autobiography*, under the year 1729, says that Bradford, the postmaster of Philadelphia, refused to allow his paper to be sent by post. Carey has an implied charge of a similar nature against that dignitary of 1792.

[12] "While the upper rooms of this building (the hospital at Bush Hill) are filled with the sick and the dying, the lower apartments are the scenes of carousals and mirth. The wretches who are hired, at enormous wages, to tend to the sick and convey away the dead, neglect their duty, and

history of the epidemic in *A Short Account of the Malignant
Fever, Prevalent in the Year 1793, in the City of Philadelphia.*
The *Short Account* was one of the most popular of its author's
works. It reached at least eleven editions. It was printed in
French at Philadelphia, in German at Lancaster, and in Dutch
at Haarlem, all in the same year, 1794. A large part of the
second edition, which appeared only twelve days after the first,
was sent to Europe to show creditors there the reasons for
non remittance. As a history based on documents, and aiming
at accuracy alone, it lacks the vividness found in *Arthur
Mervyn;* and it has none of the unforgetable incidents that
fill the pages of Defoe's *Journal of the Plague Year.* Yet
Carey appreciated the great human drama going on around
him. "Arthur Mervyn," he writes, "gives a vivid and terri-
fying picture, probably not too highly colored, of the horrors
of that period." During this time he was not a mere idle on-
looker or a dilettante writer analyzing the agonies of his suffering brother man, but an active worker in two important committees whose members were dying around him in the discharge
of their dangerous duties. Tho he was always ready to give
the best side of human nature, to choose the brightest examples, the impression he produces is one of horror yet not
the horror produced by the trained literary artist, but that
which is inherent in the subject.

After his duel with Col. Oswald, Carey's life, while at the
other extreme from ease, was at least peaceful until William
Cobbett, intoxicated by the eloquent pages of Tom Paine,
came to Philadelphia in 1792. For a while he supported himself by giving lessons in French. One day a French pupil read
a diatribe against England instead of his usual lesson. This
moved Cobbett to write a pamphlet in defense of his country.
Quite naturally for a man of his ability and aggressiveness he
soon found himself allied to the Federalists, who were friendly

consume the cordials which are provided for the patients, in debauchery
and riot." (*Arthur Mervyn,* Philadelphia, 1857, Vol. I, p. 184.) It seems
hardly necessary to refute this. All evidence now accessible points to the
fact that controlled as it was by Carey, Rush, and other citizens of un-
questioned integrity and ability the hospital was as near a model as the
medical science of that day could make it.

to England. About this time Dr. Joseph Priestley also had come to America, and Cobbett took occasion to attack him in *Observations on Priestley's Emigration*, which is, in fact, an anti-revolutionary tirade. The *Observations* were taken to Thomas Bradford, the printer; but he, being an ardent enemy to Great Britain, refused them. Cobbett then offered them to Carey, and it was thru his refusal that their quarrel first began. Immediate hostilities were occasioned by the opponents of Cobbett bringing Carey's name into their pamphlets. Some correspondence ensued between the two men, and the threatened controversy seemed in a fair way to be healed when John Ward Fenno[13] attacked Carey, who was a Democrat, thru the columns of his *United States Gazette*. The article was copied by Cobbett in his *Porcupine's* Gazette.[14] Carey's remonstrances were met by an angry answer, and Fenno's squibs continued to be copied. In the controversy that ensued Carey wrote and published the two pamphlets, *A Plum Pudding for the Humane, Chaste, Valiant, and Enligtened Peter*

[13] John Ward Fenno succeeded his father as editor of the *Gazette of the United States*. Carey calls him "a rash, thoughtless, and impudent young man." The *Gazette* was the medium thru which John Adams, when vice-president, whiled away his time and softened his disgust at his official position in a series of articles entitled "Discourses on Davilla" being an analysis of Davilla's *History of the Civil Wars of France in the 16th Century*.

[14] *The Political Censor*, a monthly which ran for eight numbers had been Cobbett's chief organ; but monthly attacks seemed too far between for this militant spirit, and so on February 1, 1797, he issued proposals for *Porcupine's Gazette and Daily Advertiser*, which ran nearly three years. Cobbett claimed in after years that he was mainly influential in keeping this country from joining France in the war then waging, and it is probable that he did exert considerable influence. Not content with political warfare, Cobbett entered the medical controversy centering around Dr. Benjamin Rush's method of curing the yellow fever by severe bleeding. The Doctor brought suit for libel because of Cobett's attacks in the *Rushlight* and elsewhere. The verdict of $5000 against Cobbett ruined him financially, and was the chief cause of his return to England in June, 1800. (See appendix I, page 114.) Those Americans who mourn over the loss to our literature when Sandys, Clough and others departed, and who speculate over the might-have-beens had the ancestors of Hunt and Shelley seen fit to remain in America, are strangely ungrateful for the very tangible four or five volumes of virile prose which Cobbett presented us.

Porcupine and *The Porcupinead; a Hudibrastic Poem,* 1799.
The title page of the former has a cut of a porcupine hanging
from a street lamp. This closed the controversy, as far as
Carey was concerned. In 1815 we learn from their correspondence that the two former enemies are now coöperating
in the cause of liberty,[15] for during the period between 1800
and 1815 the political opinions of Cobbett have radically
changed: from a Tory he has passed to the most ardent of
Liberalists. As a reformer of the ballot, as an advocate of
agricultural interests and as a bitter opponent of a standing
army he sought and obtained the aid of Carey. Both men
coöperated in opposing the reactionary tendencies which vis-
ibly followed the Congress of Vienna.

[15] See Appendix, I, p. 114 ff.

CHAPTER II

MATERIAL CONDITIONS OF PUBLISHING AND DISTRIBUTING AT THE END OF THE EIGHTEENTH AND BEGINNING OF THE NINETEENTH CENTURY

When the firm of Mathew Carey was established in 1785, printing in America, while not exactly in its infancy, was yet hardly able to maintain itself without aid from Europe. The first printing press manufactured in America was made at Germantown in 1750. At the same place, in 1772, the first regular foundry for casting type was built by Christopher Sauer (or Sower), with implements imported from Germany and intended solely for German types. Three years before, Abel Buel of Connecticut had manufactured a few fonts of long primer, but this was the first regular foundry.[1] Yet for two and a half centuries before 1785 the Americans could boast of books printed in the New World. According to the Archbishop of St. Domingo a book called *The Spiritual Ladder* was published at Mexico in 1532. No trace of it has ever been found; but Señor Icazbalceta, our highest authority on such points, thinks that such a book really was issued about 1537. There is no doubt, however, that a *Breve y mas compendiosa doctrina Christiana en lengua Mexicana y Castellana* was published in 1539.[2] This publication antedates by just an even century the first printing north of Mexico, *The Freeman's Oath* and an *Almanac calculated for New England, by Mr. Pierce, Mariner*, printed by Stephen Daye at Cambridge[3] on a press which the shrewd president of Harvard had added to the equipment of his college when he married the widow of

---

[1] Isaiah Thomas, *The History of Printing in America*, Albany, 1874, Vol. II, p. 27.

[2] Richard Garnett, Art. "Early Spanish-American Printing." In *The Library*, London, 1900, Vol I, p. 140.

[3] Samuel A. Green, *Ten fac-simile reproductions relating to New England*, Boston, 1902, p. 13.

a printer who had died on the passage over. The first real book, however, was the *Bay Psalme Book* which Daye printed the next year. In 1675 John Foster set up the first press in Boston.[4] William Bradford, of Leicester, England, established the first printing press in Philadelphia, in 1682. Religious disputes caused him to withdraw to New York, where in 1693 he set up the first press in that city.[5] Three years before the first paper mill had been erected at Germantown, a place which seems very prominent in the early history of printing in America. In 1710 the second was established there also.[6] One hundred years later there were one hundred and ninety-five, of which Massachusetts had forty and Pennsylvania sixty. Of this number seven were within Philadelphia, which in the same year could boast of fifty-one printing houses, and one hundred and fifty-three printing presses. Boston had established the first Anglo-American newspaper, in April 1704, and on December 21, 1719, had preceded Philadelphia by one day in the establishment of a second.[7] Before 1740 Massachusetts printed more than all the other colonies combined, and not until about 1760 had they equalled her output. New York and Connecticut produced a few volumes, and in Virginia and Maryland a few books were artistically printed. After about 1760 Philadelphia became a serious rival for Boston; and commercial and political supremacy soon decided the matter in favor of the former.

It was, then, to the most progressive and flourishing city in the country that Mathew Carey came in 1784, and there began alone to build up the business which was to be of so much benefit to American authors and readers. Colonel Oswald, who viewed his operations with a jealous eye, had forced him to pay more than the price of a new one for a second hand press, and his capital was practically nothing; yet in a few years he was able to make the statement that from 1792 to 1799 he did business to the amount of $300,000, and that he frequently employed for months at a time as many as one hundred and fifty

[4] Green, p. 17.
[5] Henry O. Houghton, *Early Printing in America,* Montpelier, 1894, p. 23.
[6] Thomas, Vol. I, p. 20.
[7] Ibid., Vol. II, p. 7.

men at printing. The proceeds of two works alone published at this period, the very popular Guthrie's *Geography* and Goldsmith's *Animated Nature,* amounted to $60,000 or more. The 2500 copies of the former retailed at $16.00 and 3000 of the latter at $9.00. As already noted, one of Carey's reasons for the discontinuance of the *Museum* was the increase of his business as publisher and book dealer. In a letter to his brother, Rev. Mr. Carey of Dublin, May 14, 1792, he writes:

" . . . My situation never promised so fair as at present. I have lately entered pretty largely into the printing & bookselling business. I have printed a considerable number of books on my own acct—the history of New York—Necker on religion—Beauties of Poetry—Beatties morals—Ladies' Library—Garden of the Soul—Douay Bible—McFingal, & several smaller works. I am this day going to put to press the Muses' Magazine—& as soon as I can procure paper fit for the purpose shall print Blair's lectures in two large octavo volumes.

"I have written to London, Dublin & Glasgow for a supply of foreign books without which I cannot have a proper assortment . . . ."

From this comparatively modest beginning, Carey had by 1820—about the time when Philadelphia began to lose her proud preeminence as the literary and commercial center of America—built up a trade that extended to all parts of the United States and had regular exchanges in several parts of Europe and South America. Even during the war of 1812, a period second only to the Revolution in its deterrent effects upon the spread of literature, and still more conspicuous for its dearth of creative writers, the business of the firm was fairly extensive. The exchange book for June 12, 1813, to February 23, 1814, for example, shows how widespread Carey's exchange list was, especially towards the north. At New York City there were fourteen correspondents, at Boston sixteen, and in proportion at other places, some of them now never heard of in connection with the publishing trade.[8] That

[8] The early immigrants were in many cases comparatively well educated; and wherever they went it was but natural that they should demand reading matter and attempt to supply that demand. There were as yet no central

16

the South is not represented more frequently in the exchange books is not due, as yet, so much to the fact that the South read less, tho that is probable, as to the comparative scarcity of printing presses and to the large number of branches and subscription agents maintained there. The statement has been made that more fine books were sold in antebellum times in Charleston, South Carolina, and Nashville, Tennessee, than in any other cities of the United States. Even as early as 1809 we have a demand for fine bindings from a branch at Dumfries, Virginia. However this may be, the following sentence occurs in a letter to Washington Irving March 2, 1841, concerning the publication of a volume of poems by Miss Davidson: " The great quantities however that formerly sold when the South & S. West were opened, cannot now be managed."

At the end of the eighteenth century and the beginning of the nineteenth the distributing of the products of the press presented a grave problem partly solved today by wide advertising, by the publishing of trade lists, and by rapid communication. The exchange lists referred to above were obviously one of the best means of keeping a full and varied supply of books. No publisher had yet attempted anything like the comprehensive series or libraries issued today. Indeed the choice of books—I speak of the period before Scott, Dickens and other British novelists were republished by a dozen firms as soon as the first number could be secured—seems very arbitrary; and tho the works issued were of the same general class it was obviously impossible for one publisher to cover the entire field of staple English reprints. Hence the method

places which overshadowed all lesser ones as publishing and distributing centers. Labor had not yet sought a special market, and rapid communication had not drawn outlying towns together. Therefore when a printer made his way into a small village and set up his shop, orders for printing work of all sorts came to him in fair abundance from the districts nearby. To judge by the evidence at hand, Reading, Lancaster, and Germantown in Pennsylvania, Brattleboro, Vermont, Cambridge, Massachusetts, Hartford, Connecticut, and Burlington, New Jersey were very early fairly well known to the publishing trade. Pittsburg and Cincinnati also come in for some notice at a period when they must have been hardly more than mere villages. Dumfries, Virginia, and Whitehall, North Carolina, were distributing stations of first rate importance.

of offering a certain number of books in exchange for others
became the most usual way for the larger dealers and the publishers to maintain a full stock. Once in the hands of the dis-
tributors the problem was to get them to the more remote
districts. Bad as communication was in America, it seems to have
been considered good by new arrivals. On November 9,
1789, Carey writes to his brother: "I have traveled a great
deal of late; not less in the three months of July, August and
September, than 1300 miles. In three weeks of the last month,
I rode 650 miles, on a horse that cost me only 22 dollars.
Hardly in anything is there so strong a difference between the
inhabitants of this Country & those of England & Ireland, as
in their ideas of travelling. A journey of 2 or 3 hundred miles
here is less thought of, than an excursion of forty or fifty
miles in Ireland. I made slight preparation for the journey
and the total expense of the 650 miles was not over £8. . . . "
The object of this journey, no doubt, was to secure subscribers to the *Museum* and to collect accounts. It may be
taken as typical of what a large number of canvassers were
doing; conspicuous among whom, at a later date, was the
Rev. Mason L. Weems of Virginia, author of the story of
George Washington and the hatchet, lives of Marion, Penn,
Franklin and others. By such means an immense number of
Carey's quarto Bible, Guthrie's *Geography*, Goldsmith's *Animated Nature* and Lavoisne & Versey's *Atlas* were distributed
over all parts of the country, especially thru the South and
Southwest. The woes attendant upon the book canvasser in
the twentieth century were not unknown in the first quarter of
the nineteenth as is shown by the following letter, which inci-
dentally exemplifies something more important—the attitude
towards the productions of American scholarship:

"BALTIMORE 10th Oct. 1817.
"MESSERS M. CAREY & SON.
" . . . Apropos, I could but mentally laugh the other day
when you inquired of a person how many subscribers he had
gained & how long he had been in Philadelphia. He answered
60 or 70 a week. I suppose he had a prospectus for a Bible,
a Dictionary, and Directory, Robinson Crusoe, a News Paper

3

or an Almanac, which every one were willing to possess (even then he would have been industrious.)

"But Sir, with Dr. B's Botany how would the case have been?

"You may in mind assimilate my business to water running down hill, but let me tell you it would be more just if you compared it to a shad climbing a pine tree.

"In the first place there isn't more than 1 to 500 who knows what Botany is, that one you've to search for (once in 3 mos. you may find him *unengaged* at home) then you have to convince him of the utility of an *American* production of this kind (for many possess extensive histories of exotic plants), after put down his prejudices against subscription & at last wait the will and pleasure of his *whole* family (when composed of girls more easy) and should success attend you, you in verity Pat git *one whole subscriber!*"

The names of subscribers to costly works were generally, after the British fashion, printed and bound in with the volume, a subtle way of making vanity pay tribute to the printer. John Kelley writes from Calcutta, India, February 24, 1792, about a new subscriber to the *American Museum:* "Only subscribe John Andrews, Esqr. Calcutta Bengal pretty close to General Washington or Dr. Franklin and you may charge at least 50 per cent more than you otherwise would for the Books." And this too of a man whose "knowledge of books and reading is extensive."

Freight charges are rather hard to determine. There are many entries, but the weight is never specified. In 1812 it cost twelve and one half cents per foot to send boxes of books by water to Baltimore and ten cents to New York City. At this time transportation by water was, of course, much cheaper than by land; and we find, even in many small orders, instructions given to send by boat rather than by the much quicker but more costly stage coach, which was reserved for a later day, when every publisher was trying to issue the first number of the latest British novel.[9] In 1818 the cost of getting two

[9] In 1836 Carey & Hart hired all the seats in the mail stage in order to place five hundred copies of Bulwer's *Rienzi* on the New York market before the Harper edition could appear. (J. C. Derby, *Fifty Years Among Authors, Books and Publishers,* New York, 1884, p. 551.) This, says Mr.

boxes of books, value 2100 francs, from Paris to Bordeaux and clear of the harbour was 125.50 francs, of which however only sixty were actually carrying charges between the two cities.

Up to about 1800, beyond the occasional letters between the different publishers and the exchanges referred to above there had been no attempt at coöperation, nor was there need of any. Not enough large firms had developed to clash seriously with each other by issuing too many editions of the same work. Most publishers did a strictly local business, and the remoteness of Carey's greatest rival, Isaiah Thomas of Boston— *"le Didot des États-Unis"*—had prevented any serious interference. Moreover while Carey issued many original works of great value, Thomas confined himself largely to those already tested by previous publication, the demand for which would justify simultaneous editions by other firms. About this time, and in some cases a little earlier, a few of the more enterprising firms, as Mathew Carey and Benjamin Franklin of Philadelphia, Hugh Gaine of New York, and Samuel Hall, Greenleaf & West, and Thomas & Andrews of Boston began to issue hand lists of their own publications and those of other publishers, and also of importations.[10] To an outsider seems due the first idea of a permanent organization to reduce the confusion to harmony. In the correspondence received for 1800 occurs the following undated letter.

"Great complaints have been made that the works of the most celebrated Europeans, or of the Antients, are not to be found in the United States—this is the complaint of Men of Letters.

Henry C. Lea, was frequently done many years earlier by Carey & Son. On the same page as the above reference Derby says that one day James Fenimore Cooper came to Carey & Hart with manuscript of a novel entitled *Eleanor Wyllis* which was published anonymously; that Cooper never acknowledged the authorship of the book, which was a failure, but that Mr. Hart believed Cooper had written it. The copyright was paid to him and his receipt taken for it. Lea & Blanchard were the regular publishers of Cooper at that time. (The exact date is not given, but it is probably 1836.)

[10] The first regular book-trade catalog was issued at Boston, in 1804, under the title of *The Catalogue of all the Books Printed in the United States*. The number of volumes listed is 1338.

"Booksellers or Printers are discouraged from undertaking expensive publications for these reasons:

1. It is tedious to wait for, and expensive to obtain, subscriptions.

2. If a work be undertaken without subscriptions, it is not probable that a sufficient number would sell in any reasonable time to pay the expences, unless they are distributed among the Booksellers in the Chief Cities over the Continent.

"If they should be so distributed it must either be on Commission, or exchanged, or Sold. All these methods are liable to objections. The booksellers are well aware what these objections are.

"Here then there exists great difficulties in the publication of valuable and expensive works.

"Are those difficulties to be removed? I say yes. But how? Turn over and I will tell you. Let a few of the principal Booksellers (men of credit and some wealth) in each State erect themselves into a Company to be called The Company of Stationers of North America.

"The object of such an institution would be to assist each other in the sale of these books and in making to each other expeditious remittances.

· "This would be accomplished by

1 admitting none in the corporation in the first instance but men of known probity, and possessed of Capital.

2 by forming a small joint Capital in each State for the assistance of deceased members (*sic*) or their widows.

3 by having a Common hall called Stationers Hall (with a Clerk) in each State to keep an account of the transactions between that State & the other States.

4 By regulations to prevent interference in the same work.

5 By making the terms of admission difficult such as being apprenticed to one of the society and other requisites.

6 By the expulsion of a member for infidelity to the Society or its members.

"The present State of the morals of Booksellers in the United States requires something of this kind to keep them honest punctual & willing to serve each other. If in process of time Men should grow better, there would be no occasion for associations. We must fit ourselves and our institutions to the times, since we cannot alter the Manners and Morals of Nature in a sudden.

"I am told that in general 500 copies of any book will pay the expenses and a decent profit, if so, what a vast number of books must be reprinted if booksellers would only be punctual and honest to each other.

" When this scheme[11] takes place I expect to be appointed Clerk to the Stationers Comp. of Philadelphia and perhaps Secretary to their federal meeting.

[11] It is interesting to compare this plan with what may have suggested it, The Stationers' Company of England. On July 12, 1403, those citizens of London interested in the production of books petitioned for and obtained the right to form themselves into a guild or fraternity. When the scriveners were superseded by printers the latter sold their sheets to a separate class called stationers. This class took the lead of the printers and associated their name with the guild which soon became known as the Company of Stationers. An ordinance of the city required that all persons carrying on the business of stationers or a kindred trade must enroll themselves as members and become subject to its by-laws. Every member was required to enter in the Clerk's book the title of each book or "copy" which he claimed as his property to avoid disputed ownership. This is the germ of the modern copyright. At first the craft had very narrow means; and to provide funds for an undertaking of any magnitude, several often combined. The printing in such cases was under the direction of wardens who divided the profits, a small portion being set aside for the relief of distressed craftsmen. Gradually the craft acquired wealth and power, and in 1556 it was incorporated under the title of the Masters and Keepers of Wardens and Commonality of the Mystery or Art of a Stationer of the City of London. The by-laws of the company set forth at this time include among other provisions, the following: " No printing presses to be erected without first acquainting the Master and Wardens; prohibition to all parties, abettors, and assistants against erecting ' a press in a hole' and buying pirated books; No member to suffer an apprentice to work at unlawful presses or work; no printer to teach his Art to any but his son or apprentice; no printer who works at an illegal press or on piratical books to be admitted as a pensioner; Law books to be printed by none but the patentees; No Member of the Company to print any unlicensed books; Members privy to the printing, binding or selling unlicensed publications to disclose them to the Master and Wardens on pain if stockholders of having their dividends sequestered, and if not stockholders to be fined; Pensioners offending to lose their pensions and holders of loan money to have their loans called in; Printers offending to have no stock work for one year; Those who enter copies to be reputed the proprietors and to have the sole printing of them; Penalty for printing importing or publishing another person's entered copy; Power to the Master and Wardens to search printing houses, warehouses, and shops; No entered copy to be printed by another without assignment." There was an attempt to limit the number of apprentices, but the provisions were not very strictly adhered to. In 1598 the Company took measures to limit the excessive price of books. (Charles Robert Rivington, article, " Notes on the Stationers' Company "

" A man is a bad carver if he neglect to cut a slice for himself. LITHJON."[12]

At the top of the letter Carey has written " An Idea." This idea he appears to have utilized, in part, in the following year, when in December circulars were sent out to all the booksellers and printers in the United States pointing out the immense advantages to literature and art that would be derived from a literary fair such as existed at Leipsic and Frankfort. Yearly meetings were to be held alternately in Philadelphia and New York. Carey drew up a constitution; the first meeting was held at New York, June 1, 1802, and Hugh Gaine was elected president.[13] The title of the organization was The American Company of Booksellers. All publishers and booksellers were invited to attend and bring samples of their work or of books they desired to exchange. The project was enthusiastically received, especially by those of the coast towns, where the water furnished an easy and cheap method of transportation. For a few years success attended the plan, but soon an unexpected evil overtook it. The less important and more remote publishers produced large editions of popular works on cheap paper and with worn and broken type, with which, by means of the exchange, they flooded the country. Naturally the more prominent publishers, the leaders in the company, who had in many cases good editions of these books on hand, soon withdrew, and the movement collapsed. It had however produced one very substantial benefit. In 1802 a $50 gold medal was offered for the best printer's ink, the sample to be large enough for practical publication. The same reward

in *The Library* New Series, Vol. IV, London, 1903, pp. 355–66. Compare Henry B. Wheatley, article " The Stationers' Registers " in *The Bibliographer*, London, April, 1882, pp. 130–35, and May, 1892, pp. 171–75.)

[12] This signature is a complication of flourishes. It appears to read as above, but perhaps it is Littlejohn.

[13] Mathew Carey, *Autobiography*, in *The New England Magazine*, Boston, 1834, Vol. VI, p. 306. A. Growoll, *Book-Trade Bibliography in the United States in the XIX Century*, New York, 1898, p. iii, says that the organization was accomplished in 1801, that owing to the epidemic of yellow fever the New York booksellers could take no part in the meeting of this year, and that Mathew Carey was the first president.

was given in 1804 for the best paper and also for the best binding in American leather. In other words a systematic attempt was made to improve the materials of American printing.

Noting the enthusiasm displayed in the organization of the American Company of Booksellers the school-book publishers united about 1802, under the title of The New York Association of Booksellers. "To lessen the number of imported Books" their constitution reads, "which are now becoming exceedingly advanced in price," they "have associated themselves for the Purpose of giving correct American Editions of such elementary works as are in general use in our Schools, Academies, and Colleges; and also for the publication of such other Books as may be interesting to the Community or conducive to the advancement of general knowledge." The suggestion came from Baltimore thru Boston.

"BOSTON, April 5th, 1802. (Recd. Apr. 12)
"Sir—

"Can we not, by establishing a Company or Association of Booksellers in each great commercial city, under uniform regulations, to correspond regularly with each other, by Committee, or otherwise, promote the interest of the whole, and not only multiply the number, and increase the reputation of American Editions—but prevent the importation of all such Books as may be printed by each association agreeing that as soon as any work reprinted by any member, in a manner which they approve of, no one shall be at liberty to import the same work, unless in a larger and more costly form. In our opinion the best way to prevent the importation of Books will be to improve American Editions, by making them equal to the European and this can easily be done by the booksellers each regulating their several branches of business. Let the Booksellers agree to employ none but regular bred reputable Printers to do their work at a fair price. Let the Book-Printers for the good of their art, determine to have their work well executed, and to employ none as Journey men but the few who have regularly acquired their business. And in order that the Binding may be equal to the Paper and Printing, let the Booksellers determine not to employ any but regularly bred Bookbinders and they none but regular Journeymen, except such as may already be in business. Some regulations of this nature among the three Branches would insure good Editions and there would be a certain Sale for every Book of Merit, if the Bookseller was sure that as soon as he provided a handsome Edition of all the valuable classic and School Books, in the different places, and by interchanging we should each have an assortment of valuable Books at the first cost. That measures of this kind, if they can be carried into effect, would be of immense benefit to the several branches of the business, and tend powerfully to prevent the importation of Books, we are fully convinced—how far they are practicable we do not know—but we are fully of opinion that the most important part of such a system might be carried into complete effect here.

"The preceding ideas were suggested by a circular letter from Baltimore wishing the Booksellers, etc to unite in a Petition to Congress for additional duties on imported Books. Such additional duties, we are apprehensive, would be productive of much public inconvenience, as it would be impossible to specify particular Books, and it would be a great while before all the books wanted could be printed here. Besides if we can only agree among ourselves, we can print and sell cheaper than they can be imported and sold.

"We wish you would take the preceding into serious consideration, and present to the trade, in the principal cities, the outline of a plan for improving our own and preventing the importation of imported Books. By well directed efforts we think something of the kind may be brought about.— THOMAS & ANDREWS."

On April 26, they again write: "We will endeavor to prepare the outlines of a plan for an association of the trade and wish you not to fail of attending it, as you will be able to suggest many ideas that will not occur to us. . . ."

I am unable to find the exact fate of the New York Association of Booksellers, but it seems to have been very similar to that of the American Company. At any rate only ten years later Carey is again writing to a fellow publisher about another association of a very similar nature, except that the exchange feature and a limited membership are emphasized. In spite of their brief duration, the two organizations cannot be regarded as unfruitful. The results of the former have already been glanced at: to the latter is undoubtedly due much of the impetus, to be noticed later, in school book publication and in the reproduction of the ancient classics. The feeling of coöperation and of mutual esteem that seemed to be growing up among publishers and dealers was to be almost completely destroyed at a later date by the advent of the popular novels of Scott and other British authors.

The hand lists issued by the better firms[14] were among the first steps towards the familiar twentieth century method of book distribution thru wide advertising. They were, however, largely intended for the trade. Yet as early as June 17, 1789, Carey pays to *The Freeman's Journal* a bill of £9/1/3 for inserting six advertisements, which no doubt were intended for the public at large. The neglect of advertising in general, and of newspaper advertising in particular, was a source of much discontent to editors. How great that neglect was may be judged from the comparatively infrequent entries in the following bill, which, it must be remembered, was the entire expense of the most aggressive publisher of the day.

"Mr. Mathew Carey to Andw. Brown[15] Dr.

1794			drs.	cts.
January 7th	To Advertising respecting Algerine Robbers 6 times		1	50
9th	To do........do........do ¼ squares 6 times		1	87½
16th	To do respecting The Malignant Fever 8 do		1	90
24th	To do Collection of Maps	6 do	1	50
Mar 1	To do Love in a Village	3 do		90

Up to August 6 the total was $84.64. It is noteworthy that in this bill the advertisement of *Charlotte Temple* is the third largest item. Possibly the immense vogue of that novel was due, in a measure, to persistent advertising. *The New System of Modern Geography* was advertised to the extent of $43.80; on Guthrie's *Geography*, however, only $3.93 was expended.

This neglect was not caused by lack of results; for Winifred Gates, whose commission sales were large, writing from Raleigh, North Carolina, in 1800 says that tho the last assortment was a very unsalable one she would "immediately advertise them, by giving the Title of each Book in the Paper, and if anything will sell them this will."

Moreover the *Port Folio* magazine, which was established at Philadelphia in 1801, soon found itself too freely utilized as a

[14] See p. 19.
[15] Very probably the advertisements were in Brown's *Philadelphia Gazette*.

gratuitous advertising medium. Evidently the editor thought himself abused, for in a very few years he was compelled to protest. He understood also the service of such a medium as his for bringing order out of the chaos that for a while followed the collapse of the two publishing associations, since later we find him telling the booksellers that if they would only send him notices of projected volumes there would be less confusion and fewer rival editions. Finally the book announcements and reviews became one of the most important features of the magazine. About 1819 the *North American Review* also became prominent in this way.

Everyone knows that from its very beginning to the present day there has been a constant tendency to lessen the cost of literature to the consumer. It is not necessary here to enter into the progress of mechanical science to which this result is most largely due. The prices paid by the publisher, even a century ago, were quite different from those now prevailing. From the wealth of material at hand the following bills are taken as typical of the different charges of representative periods:

FEBY 5, 1787. MR. MATHEW CAREY TO CHᵃ. CIST

To composing one sheet of his museum in small pica 27 × 48	£3/17/6
printing 1080 1/17/6	5/15/0
45 quires of paper for the same	1/17/6
To 12 reams of demy paper 15%	9/0/0
	£20/9/6

PHILADELPHIA MR. MATHEW CAREY TO DANIEL BROENTIGEN

1793 January 12 To full binding & filleting 50 Think Well on't	£1/11/3
" " " do letter & filleting @ 7½, 3 Setts American Museum 12 vols each @ ⅔	4/16/0
" " 17 To binding in Embossed paper 100 History of Charles Grandison @ 11ᵈ	1/13/11
" " 21 To full bind. letter & filleting 50 Moral Science ⅕	3/10/11

Philadelphia 19th July 1794
Mr Mathew Carey to James Hardie

To reading ½ sheet Roderic Random		1	6
To do ½ Edwards on the Affections		1	6
To 1½ days employed in correction the longitude etc.	1	2	6
	1	5	6

M. C. To William Barker,
1795

Jany. 29 To engraving a map of South Carolina[16]   £30 11 3
May 26 To   do   1 copper plate (West part of United
         States 1172⅙)   42 5 7½
Aug. 6 To   do   1 do Likeness of Muir & Palmer
         (plate incl.)   1 0 3
Mar. 12 To furnishing vallance with plate for N. C. 1 8 0

On September 15, 1800, a letter from Mount Holly referring to a cap octavo Greek grammar says:

"By putting the Notes in Brevier, the whole may be done page for page 14½ sheets, 19,000 ems in a sheet at 100 cents per 1000; which with the additional charge for Notes will bring the composition to 20 Dolls a sheet.—14½ sheets at 20 is 285 Dolls—The press work as usual."

In October, 1808, one of the friends of Carey had a book which was about to be preceded by a rival edition and he called upon him for aid. His estimate is:

"One third of the book is notes which should be done on Nonpareil, & the text in Long Primer. In that case it will make little more than 300 pages, if so much. The paper should be at least 4 dollars (Wieath's is 3:45). In that case the expense of printing 3000 copies would be $1212 for

	1000 copies.		*for 3000 copies.*
	120.00 paper at 4.00		360.00 paper
	192.00 Case Work, at 40 cents		192.00 case
	40.00 Press Work, at 4 cents		120.00 press
	180.00 Binding, at 18 cents		540.00 Binding
1000	532.00	3000	1212.00
	53¼ for 1000 each		40 cents each for 3000

In which estimate the composition is rated at 400 pages on account of notes, which will be about 10 percent too much & the notes have been counted as if done in Brevier, the text in Small Pica; . . ."

[16] For Guthrie's *Geography* 4to. August 5, 1793, Carey had offered Jeremiah Belknap three dollars a page for an article on Massachusetts. Washington, at Carey's request, lent him several hundred maps to be used in preparing this work.

Aug. 24, 1815 Mr. M. Carey To Wm Culloughton
To Printing 1000 Garden of the Soul.

Sm Pica 18 mo. 360 pages. 10 sheets.

ms   pages   ms

$19 \times 36 = 684 \times 360 = 246,240 \times 50 = \$123.00$

20 forms $= 8 \times 10$ tokens $\times 50$ $=$ 40.00

Philad 1mo 22nd 1820 Mathew Carey & Son To William
Brown Dr.

To printing five forms of Ivanhoe 11,500 m's and six
tokens per form   ($8.75 per form) $43.75

three forms of the Monestary 11,000 m's and ten tokens
per form   ($10.50 per form)   31.50

Two pages that was canseled 5 tokens of press work on
them   4.00
                                                      ―――――
                                                       $79.25

It will be noticed that one of the above items is "a likeness of Muir & Palmer." Up to 1819 illustrations were extremely expensive, but in that year the first lithograph in America appeared in the *Analetic Magazine* for July, 1819.[17] The cheapening of illustration thru this method led in the next decade to the immense increase in illustrations so noticeable in the magazines, and without doubt appreciably aided in popularizing literature.

Another process which tends greatly towards decreasing the price of books began to assume commercial importance about this time, that is stereotyping. The credit of being the first in America to use the process seems due to Dr. John Watts, who came to this country in 1804 or 1805. David Bruce further improved the art by inventing the planing mill. Electrotyping was not invented until the middle of the century. Up to the time of Watts and Bruce it was necessary to reset the type for a new edition or else allow it to stand at a great expense. In 1801 Carey adopted the latter method with a quarto edition of the Bible which he had prepared at a very great outlay, having paid a clergyman $1000 for additional references and having himself collated eighteen different texts.

[17] A. H. Smyth, *Philadelphia Magazines and their Contributors,* Philadelphia, 1892, p. 180. See also the *American Dictionary of Printing and Bookmaking,* article on lithography; but compare Appendix II. "In 1802 or thereabouts Carey had correspondence with Didot concerning the latter's use of a method of lithographing," says Mr. Henry C. Lea.

CHAPTER III

THE DEPENDENCE UPON EUROPE

It may be possible for colonies to have a really vigorous and important literature, but historical facts seem to indicate that as long as they must look to a mother country for political guidance and commercial aid so long will they fail to attain the first rank intellectually. Of course the fact must be taken into consideration that colonies seldom enjoy the material equipments of life which, if not necessary for a great literature, are at least very important factors in its development. American scholarship, for example, was retarded for half a century merely by the lack of a medium thru which it might express itself. Moreover, as long as one country accepts the customs and the intellectual attitude of another, there is little room for aught else than imitation; and an imitative literature has never save in the case of the Romans been of the first rank. As long as America was loyal to England there were no great national questions to be discussed in the prose of a Thomas Paine or the verse of a Trumbull or a Freneau; a political separation was necessary in order that a Mathew Carey should lay the foundation of an American system of political economy. And when the great political upheaval of the American Revolution came with its complete political division, there was not by any means the same clear-cut intellectual cleavage, for only the growth of years could change the bias of thought of an entire people. What wonder, then, that before the Revolution, and for a few decades after it, the output of the American press consisted mainly of reprints of English authors. It is true that to disregard the mature literature at hand would have been almost a crime against our intellectual development, but to favor the English at the expense of the American author was no less fatal. If it took John

Winthrop's *Journal* a century and a half to get into print,[1] what chance had many a lesser author?

While the Revolution produced an immense number of political pamphlets and poems, especially towards its beginning and near its close, it tended on the whole to paralyze the publishing industry. Practically every publishing center was, at one time or another, in the hands of the enemy, and suffered—as in the case of Germantown, which was of first importance as a paper manufacturing center—more or less material loss, not to speak of the energy turned into military channels. Isaiah Thomas for example was compelled to leave Boston for Worcester. But even here his business was interfered with, and we find him living for some time upon his farm. The supply of imported Bibles seems to have been completely stopped, and the Committee on Commerce ordered the importation of 20,000 from Holland, Scotland or from any place where they could be obtained. The order was not filled, however, for in 1782 Robert Aiken printed a large edition of the first English Bibles ever issued in America. This pious and laudable undertaking Congress approved in the same year because it was "subservient to the interest of religion, as well as an instance of the progress of the arts in this country."[2] Importations from England were stopped, and for a considerable period America was thrown on her own resources.

[1] John Winthrop's *History of New England* from 1630 to 1649, like the *History* of Bradford, was preserved in manuscript in the library of Old South Church, Boston, up to the Revolution. After quiet was restored two of the three volumes were found in the possession of the Connecticut branch of the Winthrops. These were as previously noticed (page 8) edited by Noah Webster, in 1790. The third volume remained in the church and was not discovered until 1816. While a new edition was being made, the second volume was burned, leaving only this careless edition of Webster's. (*Pioneer Literature*, edited by William P. Trent and Benjamin W. Wells, New York, 1903, p. 91.) Nor is this an isolated case: Bradford's *History of Plymouth Plantation*, Gookin's *An Historical Account of the Doings and Sufferings of the Christian Indians in New England* (and perhaps his *History of New England*) and a history of New England by William Hubbard passed thru vicissitudes that read like the adventures of a rare mediaeval manuscript.

[2] John Bach McMaster, *A History of the People of the United States*, New York, 1900, Vol. V, p. 283.

After the Revolution recovery was comparatively rapid. The demand for books of information was immediate and that for general reading shows a steady increase. Before 1790 there had been issued from Philadelphia presses the first American editions of Blackstone's *Commentaries,* an abridgment of *The Lives of the British Poets,* Leland's *Ireland,* Robertson's *Scotland,* and Adam Smith's *Wealth of Nations.* Between 1790 and 1800 appeared Paley's *Moral Philosophy,* Russell's *Modern Europe,* Robertson's *Histories,* Aristotle's *Ethics and Politics,* Johnson's *Dictionary;*[3] and also considerably before 1790, that edition of Rasselas which so soothed Dr. Johnson's ruffled temper. Shakespeare, Milton, Dryden, Pope, Richardson, Shenstone, Akenside, Defoe, and Goldsmith were popular before the Revolution, but with the advent of Mrs. Radcliffe and similar writers their popularity suffered a striking decline in favor of a host of *Abbeys, Romances* and *Mysteries.* Although a dealer at Raleigh, North Carolina, can write in 1800 that "nothing sells better here than modern law, an order for a Parcel of which I have just sent thro' Charleston to London," yet only a year later, after ordering a rather large list of substantial books she adds: "Mr. Carey will be so obliging as to send as many of the Novels as he can procure, it will be mutually our interest to keep a good collection, as the good folks here love *light* reading." The list[4] is disconcerting to those persons who seem to believe that our forefathers, wiser than ourselves, never frittered away their time over idle sensationalism. But tho this is not an exceptional list, for it may be paralleled in page after page of many account books, it must be remembered that there was another side to the question doubtless more important then than it is at the present day: if Carey had maintained a larger correspondence with Puritan New England there might have been a few more persons to write significantly as did his printer and paper maker at Easton, Pennsylvania, on March 13, 1800, "if you can

[3] Cf. McMaster, Vol. V, pp. 282–3. See also, in part, Charles R. Hildeburn, *Issues of the Press in Pennsylvania, 1685–1784,* Philadelphia, 1887, Vol. II.

[4] See Appendix III.

think of printing a Novel." Nevertheless even in New England Royall Tyler, in the preface to his *Algerine Captive*, notices in 1797 that in the last seven years "some dreary somebody's day of Doom "[5] and other works of its class had been replaced by such "*light* reading" as they demanded in North Carolina. On the whole Tyler thinks the change a good one; but he regrets that the new literature was "not of our own manufacture," and that it did not mirror American life, but presented a picture of European institutions and of moral attitudes totally at variance with our own. Our political dependence had passed away: our literary and intellectual dependence, tho changing in its aspect, was yet a controlling force.

But to one not inconsiderable element of our population dependence upon their mother land was quickly lost. The Germans, the French, and the Dutch were soon forced, thru linguistic and commercial necessities, to forget that they had another language and another civilization. The Germans had no small part in the first steps of American publishing. To them we owe the first paper mills. The first religious magazine in America was Sauer's *Geistliches Magazine,* 1764, for which Sauer himself cast the first type made in America.[6] In 1798 appeared the *Philadelphisches Magazin fur die Deutschen in America.*[7] Yet both periodicals were shortlived, and even as early as 1787 a firm which had "just set up a German & English Printing Office, Stationary & Bookstore," at Lancaster and were about to publish a newspaper were disappointed to find more English readers than German for they "sold three English books to one in German." And this too of all the regions in America was at this time the most thickly settled by Germans. It must be added that the importation of books in foreign languages was yet inconsiderable. To the French and the Dutch is traceable much less influence, tho works were printed in the language of each. Every person not of British descent who learned our speech was a clear gain in the struggle against literary subordination which was coming; for

[5] Lillie Deming Loshe, *The Early American Novel,* New York, 1907, p. 1.

[6] Smyth, p. 19.

[7] *Ibid,* p. 84.

such a person was free from the powerful influence of inherited English traditions and sympathies, and unawed by British criticism and condescension. Those who, like Carey himself, had sought America as an asylum from oppression were equally disinclined to accept dictation from across the ocean. Still less would the German, the French, the Dutch, or the Irish be inclined to send their children to England for their education, as was so often done by parents of direct British descent.

The uneducated reader is usually uncritical, enjoying alike, without inquiry into country or school, his *Charlotte Temple* or his *Mysteries of Udolpho*. But side by side with such readers there was growing up a race of scholars in America who were critical of each other and who were to be criticized by the learned men of Europe with whom they aspired to compete. Their lot was indeed hard. A Franklin might, thru sheer genius and aided by residence abroad, get a hearing; but difficult enough was the lot of the man of mere talent. If in 1911 American scholarship is yet lightly regarded in some quarters of Europe, what must have been the attitude a century and a quarter ago, when perhaps the most powerful of its countries had reached the point of sullen enmity? Practical equipment was sadly lacking,[8] but more serious still was the absence of a medium thru which an author could approach the learned public. As might be expected from the conservative nature of scholarship, scholarly publications lagged hopelessly behind literary. It must be observed, however, that it was largely the publications of learned societies and the occasional scholarly paper that suffered. Noah Webster published a popular dictionary; and the colossal *Ornithology* of Alexander Wilson was issued at Philadelphia as strictly an American work (tho doubtless the Scotch claimed full credit), on "American paper made of American rags"; but even towards this class of scholarly production, the letter quoted elsewhere[9] reflects the general attitude.

[8] Even as late as 1822 the "*Complete Woman in Wax*" ordered by the University of Transylvania (Lexington, Ky.) had to be made by "a celebrated artist at Florence"!

[9] Pp. 20–21.

4

The adverse conditions confronting American scholarship as late as 1824 are clearly illustrated in a circular by Carey *To the Members of the American Philosophical Society,* Philadelphia, April 14, 1824. The proceedings of this society, which included among its members Franklin, Washington, Jefferson, Adams, Rush, and others, and might reasonably be supposed to be one of the most progressive in America, were published in quarto form. Owing to the size of the volumes they were issued at very long intervals—nine in sixty-one years. "Under such circumstances," writes Carey, who was a member, "it is not wonderful so few communications are made to the society—the wonder is, that any authors are to be found to submit to such delays. It is no exaggeration to say, that there is more temptation to an American author to send his communications to London, Dublin, Edinburgh (and some members of the society have actually pursued this plan) or even to Stockholm, Petersburg, or Calcutta, than to the American Philosophical Society. In six months he might have a copy of his essay from any one of the three first places—in twelve from the fourth or fifth—and in eighteen from Calcutta! Four years is a tolerably fair average for the appearance of a communication in our transactions."

A few entries from Volume VII, published in February, 1818, are interesting.

No. 2 read Nov. 14, 1810	No. 7 read Oct. 1813
No. 5 read Mar. 15, 1811	No. 8 read Nov. 1809
No. 6 read Feb. 1812	No. 29 read July 1795

Volume VI was published July 1, 1809. "This" (scarcity of publications) "could not have arisen from the dearth of talents considering the number of eminent men who have flourished here during the existence of the society and also, that for a considerable time there was scarcely any similar society in the country."

As a practical publisher and bookseller Carey urges upon the society the immense advantage of publishing their transactions in octavo form: they will appear much more often, be more easy to handle, and more generally bought. "It is to be regretted that the mania for copying European examples led to publication in quarto form, so ill suited to the circumstances of this country."

This, it may be remarked in passing, was not the only venture of Carey into the scholarly world. In 1810 he had attempted to defend Sterne from the charge of plagiarism, and here as in all his writings he exhibits admirable common sense. Whether we agree with him or not—and many critics have taken the other side—he shows to what lengths the source-hunter can sometimes go. The following year he attempted the not very profitable task of pointing out the defects in *Hamlet,* especially the inconsistencies of Hamlet's character. Yet the timid and slavish mind might be none the worse for coming into contact with this honest opinion of a fearless, robust intellect. In 1826 he advocated the establishment of a college in Philadelphia in which English literature, the sciences, and the liberal arts could be taught, and for admission to which no Latin or Greek need be offered.[10] Mechanical drawings and other sciences were especially emphasized in the plan.

To add to the troubles of the scholar, there was no adequate importation law to protect him from rival editions if he should attempt to edit a Greek or Latin classic, compile a dictionary, or write a grammar. The evident need of such a law induced M. Carey & Sons to take up the matter.

"J. D. Ingram Esq. Jan. 8, 1823.

"We take the liberty to address you on the subject of the Bill reported by the Committee of Ways & Means on the importation of Books—believing that a part of it has been framed without due consideration of an important interest which will be materially affected by it.

"The General principle of the Bill making the duty a specific one meets our warm approbation, and is what we had wished for several years past to be done, but that part which relates to the importation of Books in other Languages does not. The Committee by whom that bill was reported was probably not aware of the extent to which the Manufacture of Books in the dead Languages has been, and is likely to be carried, and for the same reason which dictates the necessity for such provision for a home supply of Books in English in

---

[10] Some time before, Dr. Rush had proposed to abolish the study of the classics.

common use, must apply to the case of those in Latin &
Greek. To show you how far that department of the business
has already gone, we state that we have stereotyped Virgil
Delphini & Horace Delphini at an expense of nearly $6000.
Mr. Warner of this place had Ainsworth's Lat. Dict. stereotyped for which he paid $4500. Ovid & Caesar Delphini have
been stereotyped in New York. Graeca Minora is now stereotyping there for a house in Boston. Hutchinson's Xenophon is
doing there for us. In these seven books there has been in-
vested a capital of about $20,000. Cicero in 21 Vols. and Taci-
tus 3 Vols. have been printed at great expense in Boston.
Numerous other Classical Works are constantly printing here,
in N. York, Boston, Andover etc. All the Books used in
Academies & Schools and nearly all those used in Colledges
have been reprinted in this Country.

"The effect of the Clause referred to in the Bill now reported must be to lessen very much the manufacture of these
books as it is impossible without some duty to compete with
foreigners. In Europe the fondness for Classical Literature
& the demand for the books are very great. In this country
it is very small and can only increase by the gradual republication of Classical Books. We hazard nothing in saying that
the demand for all books[11] of every description after republication in this country is 20 times greater than when we are
dependent upon Europe for our supplies.[12] In the one case,
the Publishers & all the booksellers become interested in the
disposal of the work, as the one has his edition to sell and
naturally endeavors to interest the Trade at large. In the
other case the importing Bookseller receives a few Copies and
it is to him a matter of comparatively small importance when
they are sold.

"We believe the provisions for the duty being 21 cents per
lb. on all Books without exception when imported in sheets
or in boards would materially lessen the present rate upon
books generally and could hardly fail to give satisfaction generally. The Books now generally imported, are in the highest

[11] " Extraordinary as this assertion may appear to you, you will find it
correct by making enquiry of any person acquainted with the book-selling
Business in the two departments of Importation & Publication."

[12] Elsewhere Carey makes the assertion that tho he imported probably
as many books as any other dealer in America they never formed more than
⅙ of his trade. One order alone, from Dublin, February 26, 1795, had
amounted to £548/0/10. The next year we find him offering to salesmen
and correspondents a commission of 12½% on American works and 8⅓%
on European. This doubtless had something to do with the sales.

departments of Science, and those connected with the Fine Arts, and as their weight is generally small in proportion to their cost, they wd be admitted at a very moderate duty while those we can manufacture to an extent fully equal to the demands, as Bibles, School Books, Novels, etc will be in a great degree shut out . . ."

The effect upon the classical scholar of a total lack of protection for any scholarly work in the ancient classics was of course hardly less disastrous than it was to the publishing interests which so vigorously protest in this letter. And when we consider the bearing of the third paragraph we must in addition conclude that the spread of classical knowledge among those not professedly scholars was greatly retarded.

The letter also shows that by 1823 America had the material equipment at hand to supply her own wants. As indicated by the letter[13] of Thomas & Andrews, the publishers thought themselves able to cope with the situation as early as 1802, provided there was complete coöperation; and by 1823 we find individual firms strong enough to attempt it alone. We have already noticed that in 1792 Carey had written that a supply of imported English books was necessary to his business. During the beginnings of the book trade the publishers as well as the dealers had sought to restrict the duty on books because they were not yet capable of furnishing an adequate supply of domestic manufacture. Soon however they began to change their policy, and by 1820, when the agricultural and manufacturing interests were clashing over a protective tariff, they were loud in their demands of protection. One of the interests to suffer most heavily was that of Bible manufacturing. The English book trade at this period was greatly depressed.[14] The dealers sent hawkers to America, who canvassed the entire country in the special interest of the Bible manufacturers, selling between 700,000 and 800,000 Bibles to subscribers. Even the inadequate duty was largely avoided: for when books were published in more than one volume they

[13] See pp. 23–24.
[14] Other branches of knowledge suffered also. In 1801 a North Carolina dealer sends a large order for law books, asking for the " Irish edition as they wlll be the cheapest."

were sent to different ports and, as defective, passed almost duty free.[15] Jefferson, the advocate of non-protection, had taken the matter up in 1821, as in a letter[16] to Madison he urges the repeal of all duty on books and points out that the northern educational institutions had united for its repeal. To Mathew Carey more than to any one man in America was it due that adequate legislation was finally secured. The manufacturing industries, most of all, were suffering a severe restriction and in many cases a total cessation of their activities, while agriculture was in a very bad way. There were various theories then prevalent to account for this condition of extreme depression, a depression which wrought greater injury to Carey's native manufacturing city, Philadelphia, than perhaps to any other in the country. It was believed by some that it was but the natural result of a transition from a state of war, with its widespread employment of men, to a state of peace, in which large numbers of the temporarily unemployed were thrown upon the country. A second reason popularly advanced was the incorporation, in Pennsylvania, of forty-six banks, with a capital greatly in excess of their needs.

Carey had read very little and written nothing upon political economy. He had, however, as early as 1816 helped to organize a society, consisting of only ten members, entitled the *Philadelphia Society for the Promotion of National Industry.* The leadership of this society falling naturally upon Carey, he began to make a deep study of the subject, and to lay the foundation of an American protective system, the literature of which, so effectively contributed to by himself, was increased and enforced by his son, Henry Charles Carey (1793–1879), one of the greatest political economists America has ever produced. Commerce at this period was abundantly protected, as anyone at all conversant with our shipping industry up to the middle of the nineteenth century well knows. Agriculture, because of the lack of an European surplus, was not in need of any aid, nor was Carey himself personally benefited by any modification

[15] McMaster, Vol. IV, p. 513.
[16] Paul Lester Ford, *The Writings of Thomas Jefferson,* New York and London, 1899, Vol. X, p. 67.

of the tariff, for "by the importation of books I had never experienced the least inconvenience," he writes. Yet he entered into the defense of the embarrassed manufacturers with all his characteristic ardor. He took infinite pains to master the subject to the neglect of his business interests. Within the first twelve months of his activities he expended above six hundred dollars in journeys and in printing.

The most popular writer upon political economy at this period, and its accepted authority, was Adam Smith. Carey read Smith with great care, and it is characteristic of the man that he did not hesitate to attack his theories in spite of their years of intrenched authority. He found, he says, a "gross contradiction on a most vital point," which cast doubt upon the main thesis of Smith's system. This contradiction hinged upon the theory of "collateral branches of industry" which especially excited the animosity of Carey. He undertook in two essays to prove that when a great manufactory was forced to close, not only was the capital decreased or lost, but that the laborers could not and did not find employment in agriculture, etc., or even in kindred branches of manufacture,—that there were no "collateral branches of industry" capable of absorbing the economic shock when large numbers of manufacturing laborers, skilled in one line only, were thrown out of employment.

When Carey began to write upon political economy, he had no intention of going beyond these two essays, but they were received so favorably and so widely copied by newspapers in the East and North that he was encouraged to continue and he wrote nine more which had an equal circulation. The society behind Carey gave him fairly effective aid at this period by publishing and circulating his essays in pamphlets of from four to eight pages, in editions that ran as high as fifteen hundred. This extensive circulation, thought Carey, had an important effect in converting entire sections of the country to protection, where protection had scarcely a friend before. The society also published the series of eleven essays, together with two by another member, Dr. Samuel Jackson, in a book of two hundred and eighty pages. The career of the Philadelphia Society for the Promotion of National Industry was not, however, a very long one. After it had been in existence for about a year, the Agricultural Society of Fredericksburg published a memorial to congress containing some rather severe strictures upon what they termed the attempt of the manufacturing interests to obtain an unjust monopoly. In reply to this Carey wrote and published, in March, 1820, a pamphlet of one hundred and fourteen pages.[17] It was issued under his own name alone, for he had used stronger language in answer to what he considered the heresy of the memorial of the Agricultural Society than he thought the Philadelphia Society might care to have published in its name. He thought, however, that it should be willing to bear its legitimate share of the publishing expense of eighty dollars. The society refused to contribute on the ground that the pamphlet had not been published in its name. Carey withdrew, disgusted at its meanness, and it soon died for want of a resolute and active leader such as it had just lost. Carey now received practically no support, for in New York the cause of the protective tariff after agitation for about a year had ceased, temporarily at least, to be regarded as a paramount issue. In Boston and in Baltimore the friends of the tariff were not active. Yet Carey remained aggressively in the field and continued to write and publish on the subject with extraordinary rapidity. The address and the articles afterwards published as *Essays on Political Economy*[18] were, for instance, produced (except the preface of ten pages) between March 27, 1819, and November 21, 1821. And up to 1832, when by the victory of nullification the principles of the protective tariff suffered such a severe blow that for a time it seemed hopeless to advocate them, he continued to write and to publish for the cause with unflagging industry and ardor.

Not only did Carey receive little help at this period outside

[17] These essays by Carey and others of his of a similar character were afterwards collected by him under the title of *Essays on Political Economy; Or The Most Certain Means of Promoting the Wealth, Power, Resources, and Happiness of Nations; Applied particularly to the United States.* Philadelphia, 1822, 8vo, 552 pp. Pages 169 to 187 were written by Dr. Samuel Jackson.

[18] See note above.

of congress, where Clay was a stalwart protectionist, but he
even met active opposition. The same attitude that was
shown towards literature of British origin was manifested
towards articles manufactured in the mother country. They
were looked upon as better than those of domestic make, as
undoubtedly they were at first; and the importers who had
early built up a business were interested in perpetuating this
opinion. The public, then, needed to be enlightened in the
matter of the respective merits of American and British manufactures; and in this education of the people in things material
as well as in things intellectual, Carey played an important
part. Against his views and teachings were opposed such men
as Governor Wright of Maryland and the redoubtable John
Randolph of Roanoke, who is said to have made a solemn vow
that he would never wear, nor allow anyone connected with
him to wear, any article manufactured in America.

Just how hopelessly ignorant of and prejudiced against the
manufacturers the larger part of the public was at the period
immediately after the War of 1812 is shown by the tabulation
of the objections against domestic manufactures which Carey
gives:

" I. The demoralizing and debasing effects of manufactur-
ing establishments.
" II. Their injurious interference with commerce.
" III. The high rate of wages in the United States.
" IV. The great extent of our vacant lands, which ought to
be settled previously to the erection of manufacturing establishments on a large scale.
" V. The extortions practised and the extravagant prices
charged by manufacturers during the war.
" VI. The loss of revenue that would arise from protecting
or prohibitory duties.
" VII. The danger of encouraging smuggling by high
duties."[19]

These charges he takes up and refutes one by one. The
opposition of the agricultural states of the South was, of
course, the most potent reason why the protective system en-
countered so many reverses. Carey at all times tried to recon-

[19] *Essays on Political Economy*, Philadelphia, 1822, p. 62.

cile the agricultural and the manufacturing interests and to show how they were mutually dependent. To the fourth objection, therefore, he, in this particular essay as well as in others, devotes considerable space. He had formulated for himself, near the beginning of his career, a set of eleven political maxims, the ninth of which reads "the interests of agriculture and commerce are so inseparably connected, that any serious injury suffered by one of them must materially affect the other."[20] This sounds trite enough to us, but we are wise in our mass of accumulated experiences, and the opinions of 1819 are yet alive.

To prove and enforce his maxim Carey wrote and published in March, 1820, what he called *The New Olive Branch: Or, An Attempt to Establish an Identity of Interest between Agriculture, Manufactures, and Commerce; and to Prove, that a large Portion of the Manufacturing Industry of this Nation has been Sacrificed to Commerce; and that Commerce has Suffered by this Policy nearly as much as Manufactures.* The entire pamphlet of one hundred and thirty octavo pages (second edition, Philadelphia, 1821) is a strong plea, as the descriptive title indicates, for a union of interests between jarring classes; for perhaps Carey saw, even thus early, the great danger that threatened the Union should the animosities continue unabated—a danger which actually came with the Nullification crisis of 1832. In this crisis, too, if I may anticipate for a moment, Carey did no inconsiderable service as a peacemaker.

The entire body of Carey's writings upon political economy could probably not now be collected, for many of them were published as extremely thin and perishable pamphlets, and many others were written under an assumed name and were not all collected or acknowledged. But those that survive— probably the great majority—display such prodigious industry and productiveness as to give a feeling of discomfort to the average person. He must also come away from their perusal with a feeling of admiration for the high motives which prompted Carey to devote such a large part of his time and

[20] *Ibid.*, p. 26.

energy to a cause in which he had only a humanitarian and a patriotic interest. Few men, even when personally interested, ever show so much devotion to a losing cause thru such a long period of years. The reader must be impressed, too, by the candor and the fairmindedness of the man. At times he does indeed use language more impassioned than is supposed usually to comport with such an abstruse and impersonal science as political economy, but it is always directed towards showing the unfortunate condition of some class or community rather than towards a personal denunciation of any particular individual or interest. This turn of mind it was which particularly fitted Carey for the role of peacemaker. The "olive branch," if we judge by the number of times the expression occurs in the titles of his books, was his favorite emblem.

If the reader is at first struck by the self-assurance of Carey in taking up and writing upon such a difficult subject as political economy before he had any training in that science, he must acknowledge that he acquired a fair degree of mastery in a surprisingly short time. The abundant references to the authorities and to the original sources of his time show how carefully and how widely he had read. A favorable impression is also created by the frankness with which he acknowledges his liability to err. This trait the following passage well illustrates:

"I throw myself upon the indulgence of a public, a sincere desire to promote whose welfare and happiness has given birth to this work, which is published with a full conviction of its manifold imperfections. Let me be permitted to add, in the words of the great Chaptal—'I have neglected nothing to procure correct information. I do not, however, pretend to publish a perfect work. All that I can pledge myself for, is, that it emanates from honest intentions.' Such is the language of the Minister of the Interior of France, respecting his admirable work on 'French Industry.' If, with the immense advantages he possessed through his official station, and his unlimited command of the national statistics—he found it necessary to propitiate public opinion for the indulgence of his errors—how incomparably more necessary is such propitiation for this work, labouring as I have done, under almost every kind of disadvantage to which a writer is liable. Let me observe, as an additional reason for critical indulgence, that before I began to write the addresses of the Philadelphia Society for the Promotion of National Industry in 1819, I had never devoted three days to the study of political economy."[21]

If Carey was by nature a wielder of the olive branch, he had every need of his talent before the end of his career. The reader will recall that in 1824 the continued agitation for a protective tariff, not one for revenue only, bore fruit in a bill whose essential effect was to exclude from the American market such foreign goods as competed with those of domestic manufacture. A convention, of which Carey was a member, met at Harrisburg, Pennsylvania, in 1827 to discuss a still further increase in the duties on certain articles. The attendance from the slave states was noticeably small. Then came the famous " Tariff of 1828," which went further than any other in prohibitive duties, especially on woollen and cotton fabrics. The southern planters were alarmed lest Great Britain, by adopting retaliatory measures, should injure the exportation of cotton. As a result came the critical period of Nullification.

Carey, true to his character as peacemaker, did all in his power to relieve the tense strain which threatened civil war. In a series of ten letters addressed to Henry Clay and entitled *Prospects on the Rubicon. Letters on the prevailing excitement in South Carolina. On the means employed to produce it. On the causes that led to the depreciation of the great staple of the state. And on the misconceptions of the effect of the tariff* (Philadelphia, Feb., 1832), he endeavored to point out the lack of ground for the uncompromising attitude of South Carolina. *A Solemn Warning on the Banks of the Rubicon* followed in July of the same year. But the Nullifiers refused to take warning, and in the same month Carey published *The Crisis*.[22]

In a meeting held at Charleston in 1832 Mr. Adams' bill and that of the secretary of the treasury had both been repudiated, "because they retain the principle of imposing taxes for

[21] *Essays on Political Economy*, p. ix.

[22] *The Crisis, An Appeal to the good sense of the nation, against the spirit of resistance and dissolution of the Union.* Philadelphia, 1832.

the purpose of protection, which is a power not granted to the Constitution, and, whilst it is maintained, will continue to endanger our rights." Taking this as a text Carey proceeds to appeal for the integrity of the federal government and the submission of the states to it. He points out the two alternatives if the southern states should persist in this attitude—civil war to maintain the Union or passive submission and disintegration.

"The complaints of South Carolina," he writes, "embrace four objects: the distress said to be consequent on the protective system; the unconstitutionality of that system; internal improvements; and the colonization society."[23] Carey limits himself to the first two.

The long years of advocacy of a doctrine so bitterly repudiated by many had not been without their sting to Carey, and the dislike of a body of his fellow citizens was so bitter to him that it finally drew forth this cry:

"I have laboured in this great cause for above thirteen years—expended above 4000 dollars on it, for paper, printing, journeys, books, postage, etc., although I have never had any personal interest in it—neglected my business while I was in trade[24]—lost some of my best friends and customers—gave up my enjoyments—excited deadly hostility—was subject to abuse in and out of Congress, and in newspapers, pamphlets and stump speeches—and burned in effigy in Columbia. So far, nevertheless, as regards the public interest, I do not regret those sacrifices; on the contrary I glory in them. But as regards my personal feelings, I take heaven to witness, I have reason to curse the hour when I engaged in the cause. . . .

" . . . From the great quantity I write, it is supposed that I take a pleasure in writing. This is a great error. Writing is to me irksome, requiring an effort which is painful."[25]

The Crisis concludes with a rather remarkable epitaph, to be used if the nullifier should secede, one of the spectacular methods by which Carey often gained the attention of a wide circle of indifferent or hostile readers. The capitalization is largely omitted, and the spacing is not reproduced.

[23] *Ibid.*, p. 4.
[24] The large number of letters on political subjects among the correspondence bears ample witness to this.
[25] *The Crisis*, p. 20.

" Epitaph "

" Here, to the ineffable joy of the Despots, and Friends of
Despotism, throughout the world, and the universal distress
and mortification of the friends of human liberty and happiness,
lie the shattered remains of the noblest fabric of Government,
ever devised by man, the Constitution of the United States.
The fatal result of its dissolution was chiefly produced, by
the unceasing efforts of some of the most highly gifted men
in the U. S. whose labours, for a series of years had this
sinister tendency, by the most exaggerated statements of the
distress and suffering of South Carolina, (unjustly ascribed
to the tariffs of duties on imports) which, whatever they were,
arose from the blighting, blasting, withering effects of Slavery;
together with the depreciation of the great Staple of the State,
the inevitable consequence of over production: caused, in a
great degree, by the depression of the Manufactures of the
country, in 1816, 1817, 1818, 1819, 1820 & 1821, for want of
the protection of the government, withheld by the miserable
tariff of 1816. Here, then, at length, is the problem solved,
whether man be fit for self government: and, alas! determined
in the negative. For no country ever had, and it is utterly
improbable any country will have, equal advantages with those
we enjoy."

He further contributed to the literature concerning Nullification an *Essay on the Dissolution of the Union,* written in
September, 1832, and signed Hamilton. The pamphlet is an
eloquent appeal to the people of the South to preserve the
Union, to make it known to all nations that a government by
the people was not a thing of a season but an enduring reality,
a light to the oppressed and a rebuke to the tyrannies of the
earth.

At least three things must become evident to the person
who reads the essays of Carey upon political economy, and
such closely allied subjects as have just been sketched. He
must be impressed with the remarkable energy and industry
of the man. His grasp of his subject before he had been writing any length of time will be disputed by few, and the
patriotism and philanthropy that inspired him to such heroic
efforts must inevitably excite strong feelings of admiration.
" His energy, his high-mindedness, and his indomitable per-
severance, will force themselves upon the most casual ob-

server," wrote[26] Poe, and to no part of Carey's life does this better apply than to the period from 1819 to 1832.

To return to the somewhat more narrow issues of political economy as applied to books alone, the importation of books in foreign languages was seemingly never very large. There was a relatively small number of immigrants. Their education was, comparatively speaking, probably greater than is that of the immigrants of the present day. The absence of national prejudice on the part of the Americans permitted free inter-marriage among the whites. These conditions combined prevented those who sought new homes in America from forming communities so large and so conservative that they were still inclined to feel themselves almost a part of their mother country, demanding its literature and making no great effort to acquire a mastery of the language of the country which supported them. Such phenomena are unfortunately becoming visible today. French was not read so much as at present. Its acquisition was probably even a greater mark of culture, but it was not needed, as it is now, by the host of tourists; and few schools taught it. French immigration was never great; and that brilliant little colony at Philadelphia, of which King Joseph was the head, was merely an episode. Tho there are many letters from France in the Carey correspondence—especially during the French Revolution and immediately after[27]—very seldom are orders for French books to be found. Indeed more American books are ordered by the French than *vice versa*. It is not probable that some other dealer was supplying the country. There is no evidence that they were imported at Boston in appreciable quantities. In 1801 we find Hugh Gaine, the best known and most extensive dealer in New York, ordering from Carey himself, French books not of a technical or special character, but such as would undoubtedly be classed as "*light* reading" in North Carolina. If such books could not be obtained nearer than Philadelphia the amount of French literature bought and sold in New York must have been extremely small.

[26] *The Southern Literary Messenger,* Richmond, 1836, p. 203.
[27] These letters are generally attempts to get information about some lost friend or relative—a gruesome sidelight upon that great upheaval.

The case was very similar with German importations. The number of colonists was greater; and tho mere numbers enabled them sometimes to retain their identity, as in the case of the Pennsylvania Dutch, yet, on the whole, they were more quickly adapted to their surroundings than the French. If there was no period of a Grand Monarque for them, the former citizens of obscure little principalities, in many cases, to look back to with a pride of race that militated strongly against a loss of identity, still less was there a literature such as France possessed for them to draw upon; for the crowning achievement of German literature was yet being dreamt of at Weimar. Outside of the German born there was practically no one at the end of the eighteenth century for whom books should be imported. German was not taught in our schools,[28] and the knowledge of the language—witness the wretched translations of Schiller and Kotzebue—was small indeed. The interest of Charles Brockden Brown in German literature must be pointed out as something remarkable. In fact, as we shall see in another chapter, the balance of trade, if not in our favor, was at least equal. The Dutch were soon assimilated; and when in 1822 we find arrangements being made for a representative of M. Carey & Sons at Gibraltar we may be sure from other evidence that the Spanish importations are intended for the South American market. The dependence upon Europe then, for all but those of English descent, was a condition very soon surmounted.

[28] Frederick H. Wilkens, *Early Influence of German Literature in America*, New York (no date), Reprint No. 1, *Americana Germanica*, Vol. III, No. 2, p. 60. Blaettermann, who became professor of modern languages at the University of Virginia in 1825, seems to have given instruction in German, but the first regular instructor was appointed by Harvard, in 1826. Ticknor says that in 1813 he could not find a German dictionary in Boston, but had to borrow one from New Hampshire. (*Life, Letters, and Journals of Geo. Ticknor*, Boston, 1877, Vol. 1, p. 11.) Compare Harold Clark Goddard's *Studies in New England Transcendentalism*, New York, 1908, pp. 202–206. (Appendix, " German Literature in New England in the Early Part of the Nineteenth Century.")

CHAPTER IV

THE GROWING FEELING OF NATIONALISM AND THE RISE OF AN AMERICAN LITERATURE

Just as the Normans could not long endure political separation from France without becoming Englishmen, with a desire to build up a native literature and social and political institutions which should in some measure be their own, so the Americans soon began to feel that with a new government and new social aims they should have a new literature—one that no longer was a mere reflection of a more brilliant one across the ocean: *A Conquest of Louisburg* must be replaced by an *Eutaw Springs,* tho the change is not by any means so rapid as the juxtaposition of these two titles indicates. The quotation from Royall Tyler in the last chapter shows that in 1797 there was already a strong feeling among certain men that a national literature was necessary. Not every one however was of this opinion. Joseph Dennie, the gifted editor of Philadelphia's most brilliant magazine, *The Port Folio,* was, for instance, strongly drawn towards the mother country and resisted all American innovations as long as possible. Yet six months after his death, in 1812, we find his successor advising another editor to this effect: " We know that there has been a time, when, *merely to have been the growth of transatlantic regions,* constituted, among the people of the United States, an exalted recommendation, both to persons and opinions. Fortunately, however, for the dignity and self-respect of our country, that humiliating period is passing away. Perhaps it may be said to have already expired. We are assuming, as a people, much more of a national character, and learning to set a higher and juster value on everything comprised under the epithet *American*. . . . To contribute to the conformation and diffusion of this patriotic spirit, by giving a place, as often as possible, to valuable papers of American composition, constitutes, in our estimation, an indispensable duty of all our conductors of public journals."[1]

English critics at the beginning of the nineteenth century had looked with disdain upon the attempts of what they still regarded as an inferior people to establish a national literature, and only those Americans of considerable independence of spirit were able to resist the infection. The general public were ready for the rise of a new literature, for the amount of reading was large. Charles Brockden Brown thought that tho we produced comparatively few original books the proportion of readers was not exceeded by any country in the world.

The general public, in strong contrast with many critics, regarded the nationality of the author with considerable indifference, the evidence afforded by Cooper's *Precaution* notwithstanding; unless perhaps this case may be accounted for as peculiarly temporary in character as being synchronous with the new and widespread vogue of Scott, which for a few years did lessen the popularity of American novels. As early as 1790, however, Mrs. Rowson had published *Charlotte Temple* without attempting to conceal her identity. Its popularity was immediate and enduring. In 1812 Carey was yet able to write to her: " . . . Mentavia never was very popular. The sales of the Trials of the heart have been slow. Charlotte Temple is by far the most popular & in my opinion the most useful novel ever published in this country & probably not inferior to any published in England. The Fille de chambre is likewise popular—& the same may be said of Reuben & Rachel. . . . It may afford you great gratification to know that the sales of Charlotte Temple exceed those of any of the most celebrated novels that ever appeared in England. I think the number disposed of must far exceed 50,000 copies; & the sale still continues. There has lately been published an edition at Hartford, of as Fanning owned 5000 copies, as a chapbook— & I have an edition in press of 3000, which I shall sell at 50 or 62½ cents."

[1] *The Port Folio,* Philadelphia, 1811 (*sic*), Vol. 7, pp. 171-2 (June, 1812, number).

Nor was this a purely isolated case. As noticed previously immense numbers of Carey's *History of the Yellow Fever* had been sold, and when his *Olive Branch* appeared in 1814 its popularity was even greater; while the popularity of Brown, in the later part of his career and after his death, is well known.[2]

In one branch of knowledge the Americans were clearly better circumstanced during this period than the British—that of exploration and its attendant study of races. As early as 1770 the Abbé Raynal's book[3] had produced a sensation and had been translated into almost every European language. America was, say by the time when Scott by his advent drew away attention from everything but the novel, comparatively little known to Europeans; and in fact to the Americans themselves, for Long had but just made his expedition of discovery, and St. Louis was yet a frontier town. William Bartram's *Travels through North and South Carolina, Georgia, East and West Florida* had gone thru two editions in Philadelphia, by 1790, two in London two years later, and by 1801 had been published at Dublin, Berlin, Haarlam, and Paris.[4] Possibly in this instance the popularity in England and America was partly due to pure charm of style, but this could hardly have been the case with the other countries. The curiosity regarding a strange, new land to which many of their citizens were emigrating must have been the compelling reason for the popularity of such books. A trading upon this curiosity produced such slanderous accounts as *The Domestic Manners of the Americans* (1831), *American Notes* (1842) and many more of the same sort. When a regular system of book exchange had been established with England and Germany we

---

[2] The sale of Brown's novels was at first slow. In a letter to his brother Joseph he writes in 1800: " Book-making is the dullest of all trades, and the utmost that any American can look for in his native country is to be reimbursed his unavoidable expenses." (Ellis Paxton Oberholzer, *The Literary History of Philadelphia*, Philadelphia, 1906, p. 167.)

[3] *Histoire philosophique et politique des établissements et du commerce des Européens dans les deux Indes.*

[4] M. Katherine Jackson, *Outlines of the Literary History of Colonial Pennsylvania*, Columbia University Press, 1906, p. 148.

find that books on travel are those continually insisted upon, a demand which the American publishers are eager to meet and American writers willing and capable of filling. Offers of journals of travel are not infrequent. In 1819, D. H. Cotterel, who has spent several months at Panama and upon the "Isthmus of Darien," wants to publish a history of his travels. He writes that a Panama canal is "not only feasible but easily practicable."

The first regular interchange of books with any foreign country, as far as I have been able to find, was brought to pass thru this desire to learn about the geography and the history of America. In November, 1793, C. D. Ebeling,[5] who signs himself Professor of History and Greek at the Hamburg Gymnasium, desires to open up a correspondence with an American publishing house in order especially to get works containing the data necessary for his forthcoming history. In reply to the first inquiry of Carey as to the possibility of an opening for American books in Germany he writes: ". . . But with regard to American books, I must tell you that English is not read so universally as you seem to think. Most of the best English books are translated immediately; the Booksellers look even to American Books already in order to publish them in German. So the Description of Kentucky you sent me is already translated at Nuremburg, at Leipsig and an abridgment published at the last place also. *Bartram's* Travels are translated at Berlin. *Ramsay's* History of the Revolution also.

[5] Christopher Daniel Ebeling (1741–1817) was educated at the University of Göttingen. In 1769 he became instructor in the *Handelsakademie* at Hamburg, in 1784 Professor of History and Greek in the *akademische Gymnasium* of the same city, and in 1799 city librarian. His chief work in this last connection was the recataloguing of the library and the introduction of a more modern system. His collection of maps numbering 4000 volumes was bought by Israel Thorndike and brought to this country. He appears to have been one of the very first European authorities upon the geography and the history of America. He is the author of thirty-eight works, of which the most interesting to Americans are *Amerikanische Bibliothek* (1777–1778) in four volumes; the *Neue Sammlung von Reisebeschreibungen* (1780–90) in ten parts; and the *Erdbeschreibung und Geschichte von America*, which appeared (volume one in 1793) as part thirteen of Busching's *Erdbeschreibung*.

Of Morse's Geography three translations are announced. The Description of Tennessee would sell if the map mentioned in the title page was with it. Carleton's map I fear will not sell. The laws of the U. S. and your magazine as also the —— (illegible) will do better. . . . From your Geography not more than a dozen might not be sold, for there is immediately a translator who purchases a copy and advertises a translation for half the price. . . ."

On March 20, 1794, he says: " The public libraries of Göttingen and other universities in Germany wish to establish a regular correspondence with some active and accurate bookseller in America, by my help, and have given me order to procure them catalogues of New Books printed in America. They wish to be provided with the magazines, but only under condition of a regular continuation, avoiding defects and duplicates."

Ebeling contributed an article or so to Guthrie's *Geography*, published by Carey. He ordered American books in large numbers to use in preparing his own historical works and he also acted, without charge, as agent for Carey. He shows his true German anxiety for extreme accuracy when he tells Carey to send him copies of Kentucky, Tennessee, and western newspapers no matter how stained or torn. The entire correspondence, covering some fifty quarto pages of closely written matter, is very interesting as showing the attitude of Germany at this early period towards America. Later on, Ebeling turns the exchange over to a regular book firm, but it is interesting to note that the balance is always in favor of America.[6]

The demand for works on travel was not less eager in England. The critics there might sneer at the poetical productions of our country and at our novelists, but in this field they were disarmed by lack of information.

But something more than a mere desire for knowledge was necessary to establish literature in America and to obtain recognition for it abroad. There needed to be a deep interest among Americans for their country and a feeling that a literature was worth building up. In neither of these feelings was

[6] As an example of what the few Americans who knew German were reading in 1816, see Appendix IV.

Mathew Carey lacking. It soon became recognized that in him every aspiring author had a friend. When an enthusiast wants a new edition of the *Poems* of James Gates Percival, "the first poetical genius of this country," it is to Carey that he turns because of his "well known devotion to literature," a phrase that occurs more than once. No other publishing firm, even in proportion to its size, published so many works of native production between 1787 and 1824. As must be the case with every firm there were many requests for publication which could not be granted; but no other publishing house could, during this period, point to such a list of names as Mrs. Rowson, Noah Webster, Freneau, Percival, Irving, Weems, John Neal, Cooper, and many others of lesser importance whose works were first issued in whole or in part by this enterprising firm, which also first printed Scott and Dickens in this country. Later the firm or its direct successors published some of the first works of Poe and of Simms. Perhaps the enthusiasm of Carey for American literature inspired some of his agents to exertions in its behalf that were altogether too unrestrained. To the Rev. M. L. Weems, who never, it seems, did things by halves, it is necessary to write in 1821, "For Heaven sake do not encourage every man who has written a Book no matter whether good or bad to apply to us. You worry us to Death. We have full as much on our hands as we can manage."

In other ways than as the mere disseminator of the works of other men Carey was of great value to America. A glance at the chronology of our literature during the first decades of the nineteenth century will show how much he contributed himself towards keeping his own typesetters busy.

In 1810 the question of the renewal of the charter of the Bank of the United States came before the people. The charter was to expire on March 3, 1811, and Carey, who had acquired fair experience as a bank director, took a deep interest in the matter. For three months he dropped all his business affairs and devoted himself to securing a renewal; because he foresaw, thus early, what really happened—the disasters consequent upon the excessively large number of state and private banks founded upon fraudulent or insecure foundations, which so largely contributed to subsequent panics. The great majority of Carey's fellow Democrats were against the renewal, and so he, standing alone, was regarded as a traitor to his party and held in enmity by his quondam friends. Undaunted however by this isolation he began vigorously to uphold his opinions in a series of essays, seventeen or eighteen in number, which appeared in the *Democratic Press,* of Philadelphia, published by one John Binns, who, though personally opposing the renewal, gave Carey entire freedom to promulgate his unpopular opinions thru his paper. Thru the columns of the same paper Carey was vigorously assailed and in the *Aurora* his motives were questioned, and his character attacked. Yet, undismayed, he continued the somewhat uneven fight; for the bank directors made little effort to defend themselves or to placate public opinion.

The principal arguments used against the renewal of the charter were that it was "a National Bank," and that when re-chartered it would be under the control of the government, which did not have the power to appoint a single person, director or messenger, connected with it, and in the second place,— and argument dear to the Democrats—that it was in fact an English bank, a branch of the Bank of England.

These views, and many another of lesser importance, Carey set himself to combat. But his efforts were coldly received by the very men he sought to protect. When he applied to the cashier for information regarding some points he wished to refute, it was refused him on the grounds, as he afterwards learned, that the directors did not wish it to appear that they had any connection with him. Notwithstanding all the efforts which he made in their behalf they never gave him a vote of thanks. Carey went to Washington in person in order to influence the Pennsylvania delegation as much as possible in favor of the renewal and to convince them of the danger of a non-renewal. As he followed the debates in Congress he marked what seemed to him absurd assumptions and conclusions, and in order to expose some of these he wrote, in a few hours, with that marvelous facility in composition so characteristic of him, and had printed, a pamphlet entitled *Desultory Reflections on the ruinous consequences of a non-renewal of the Charter of the Bank of the United States.* Some unguarded assertions, made in the haste of composition, appeared in the pamphlet, which caused the offended speaker to exclude the *Reflections* from the House; but nevertheless they were widely read. Carey published three editions, which he distributed at his own expense. A second pamphlet of eighty pages, entitled *Nine Letters to Dr. Adam Seybert, Representative in Congress for the City of Philadelphia, on the subject of the renewal of the charter of the Bank of the United States,* was likewise disseminated soon afterwards.

Among other arguments, Carey drew attention to the fact that the government had sold, to private individuals, shares in the stock of the Bank of the United States some few years before and at a substantial advance. These purchases were made in full belief that the bank was to be as permanent as the Bank of England, otherwise the buyers would not have purchased at any price. If the charter were not renewed it was clear that the purchases would fall to par, and the purchasers would rightly be aggrieved at this betrayal of their trust in the honor and stability of the government. The opposition to the bank was too strong to be resisted. So strong and destructive, in fact, did the mania against banks in general become during the heated controversy, that many advocated the abolition of all state banks as well as of the Bank of the United States, without taking thought of the chaotic financial condition such a step would cause. The measure for which Carey had worked so earnestly was at last lost in February, 1811.

In the light of subsequent events, however, Carey had proved himself a wise financier, for the untoward influences of the multiplication of state banks and the general suspension of specie payments as the result of the War of 1812 showed the statesmen of the time that the restraining influence of the "old regulator," the Bank of the United States, was badly needed, and the second United States Bank was established at Philadelphia on April 3, 1816. Indeed it might be said that Carey saw his stand twice vindicated, for the panic of 1837 was largely a result of the encouragement afforded to unsound banks by the veto of President Jackson to the bill for the renewal of the charter of the United States Bank in July, 1832.

Carey has left it on record, in his *Autobiography,*[1] that he considered that the three most important achievements of his life were, the publication of the *Vindiciae Hibernicae,* the defense of the Protective System, and the publication of the *Olive Branch.* To the average American the first work is of much less interest than the last. In the *Olive Branch* Carey has treated a great crisis in American history, the internal dissensions of the War of 1812, in a vigorous and helpful way. In his pages we obtain vivid glimpses of the bitter wrong that drove our country into that struggle, and of the treacherous factionalism whose rancour brought the Union to the very verge of civil war and dissolution. We had met disaster after disaster on land. The Hartford Convention showed the danger from within; the president had called, in his message of November 4, 1812, for new and mysterious legislation against "corrupt and perfidious intercourse with the enemy, not amounting to treason," and sectional and partisan feeling was running higher than ever before or after, with one exception. Civil war was never far away. Carey's dedication to the second edition, January 4, 1815, is not overdrawn. " Go, Olive Branch, into a community, which, drugged into a death-like stupor, with unparalleled apathy beholds the pillars of the government tearing away—property sinking in value—the country prostrate at the feet of a ruthless foe, anarchy rapidly approaching, a number of ambitious leaders, regardless of the common danger, struggling to sieze upon the government, and apparently determined the country shall go to perdition, unless they can possess themselves of power; and, with this view, opposing and defeating every measure, calculated to insure salvation. Appeal to the patriotism, the honor, the feeling, the self-interest of your readers, to save a noble nation from ruin."

Carey was appalled by the violence of some of the leaders of the Federalists, the anti-administration party, who opposed the

[1] Vol. VII, p. 239.

war, and disgusted by the inactivity of the Democrats. With a mind harrowed by doubts of the continued existence of his country, he sat down on September 6, 1814, to do what he might to avert the disaster which seemed imminent. The one solution at that time appeared to be a radical change in the administration whereby the coöperation of the Federalists might be obtained by giving them a fuller share in the control of the government. This he thought might be brought about by the resignation of certain members of the administration. Carey acknowledges, on the one hand, the arrogance of this plan and, on the other, its weakness, but the situation seemed too desperate for hesitation. With this idea he began to write. Then the news came of the defeat of the British at Baltimore, of Macdonough's triumph on Lake Champlain, in the signal victory at Plattsburgh. This put a better aspect on the face of affairs, and Carey was led to believe that a candid appeal to the honor and the patriotism of both parties might even then unite them.

Yet, he writes, "I was struck with astonishment at my Quixotism and folly, in expecting to make an impression on a community, torn in pieces by faction; a prey to the most violent passions; and laboring under the most awful degree of delusion."[8] The patriotism and love of his fellow men which always so powerfully swayed Carey won the day, however.

"I should have preferred by far, for the remainder of my life, steering clear of the quicksands of politics. None of the questions that have heretofore divided parties in this country could have induced me upon the tempestuous ocean. But at a crisis like the present, neutrality would be guilt. . . .

"While I was deliberating about the sacrifices which such a publication as this requires, one serious and affecting consideration removed my doubts, and decided my conduct. Seeing the thousands of the flower of our population—to whom the spring of life just opens with all its joy, and pleasures, and enchantments—prepared in the tented field to risk, or, if

---

[8] *The Olive Branch; Or, Faults on both Sides, Federal and Democratic. A Serious Appeal to the Necessity of Mutual Forgiveness and Harmony.* Sixth Edition, Philadelphia, September, 1815, p. 30. All references are to this edition, unless otherwise specified, though the first edition of November, 1814, has been collated.

necessary, sacrifice their lives for their country's welfare; I thought it baseness in me, whose sun has long passed the meridian, and on whom the attractions of life have ceased to operate with their early fascination, to have declined any risk that might arise from the effort to ward off the parricidal stroke aimed at a country to which I owe such heavy obligations. With this view of the subject I could not decide otherwise than I had done.[9] . . . When tender women have freely gone to the stake or to the gibbet, for dogmas, which they could not understand; it does not require a very extraordinary degree of heroism, for a man of fifty-five, to run any risques, of person or character, that may attend a bold appeal to the good sense of the nation, with a view to acquire the benediction, pronounced in the declaration, ' Blessed are the peacemakers.' "[10]

Inspired by such high motives Carey took up the task more vigorously than ever. Even with his usual speed and his extraordinary capacity for work, it yet remains something of a mystery how he managed to produce between September 6 and November 8, a book the size of the first edition of *The Olive Branch,* for aside from the mere composition, the amount of research was extremely large. State documents, histories, private correspondence, and newspapers were ransacked to establish every point at issue.

The first part of the book is devoted to a review of the desperate condition of the country—a condition that should have caused every man to bury the discords of partisanship and to stand upon the broader grounds of mutual forgiveness and patriotic toleration. Then, in order that the reason for this spirit of fraternal patriotism may be clear, Carey enters into the errors that have characterized both parties. To the Democrats he charges too great fear of the federal government, opposition to the establishment of a small navy, the Alien and Sedition law, Jay's treaty, and the non-renewal of the Bank of the United States. An equally heavy bill of errors is drawn up against the Federalists.

Then apparently Carey asks himself: Is the war a just one, in defense of the people and their rights and waged in response

[9] *Ibid.,* p. 15.
[10] *Ibid.,* p. 34.

to their demand, or is it the result of narrow party interest carried on at the expense of a large and injured section of the country? He proceeds to show that in 1805 and 1806 the indignation of the people and of the mercantile interests in particular, the latter of whom were the most determined opponents of the war, was so roused by the pretensions of Great Britain to limit the trade of Americans in the colonial productions of her enemies, that they seemed almost determined to force the administration into war. Memorials of Newburyport, Salem, Boston, New York, Philadelphia, and Baltimore merchants during these two years are given in full to prove his assertion that the merchants of the country had aided very materially in placing the government in a position where war was the only logical outcome. From Newburyport to Baltimore, he asserts mercantile citizens of the United States goaded the government to a resistance of the flagrant outrages and high-handed pretensions of Great Britain. In a passage that exhibits one of the characteristic methods of the work, he turns upon one of these bodies of memorialists and says: " When the merchants of Newburyport 'Rely with confidence on the FIRMNESS and JUSTICE of the government, to obtain for them compensation and protection,' they must have been insane, if they did not calculate upon WAR as the *ultima ratio*. These are the worthy citizens who stand recorded in the annals of their country, as having since *patriotically* pledged themselves to resist their own government, 'EVEN UNTO BLOOD.'"[11] The method is, I repeat, characteristic, but the spirit of invective is most unusual in all the works of Carey, and the scarcity of such passages elsewhere shows how strongly his feelings were here aroused.

The wrongs so freely dealt out to us by a nation which seemed blindly bent upon forcing us into war, are dwelt upon at length in order that those opposed to the war may no longer say that it was unprovoked and needless. The withering effect of those futile measures of retaliation, the Non-Intercourse Act, and the Embargo acts, are shown in full.

But what of course finally precipitated the war was the impressment of American seamen; and in the cause of the sailor,

[11] *The Olive Branch*, p. 101.

who seemed then to have had all too few friends, Carey enters with characteristic warmth of heart and fullness of unimpeachable detail. Here in the dry, terse language of naval reports and of affidavits are narrated outrages and burning wrongs that yet make the blood flame. When, over the signatures of Commodore Rogers and of Commodore Porter, who quote from the log-books of the vessels concerned, it was shown that one-eighth of the crews of the Moselle and of the Sapho were impressed Americans[12] (who, too, were doubtless told that "if they fell in with an American man-of-war, and they did not do their duty, they should be tied to the mast, and shot like dogs,"[13]), the full enormity of Great Britain's crime against the law of nations must have come home to the most fanatical opposers of the war. But not content with one instance or two, Carey multiplies case after case. And yet some said that the war was not justified!

"They deride the idea of struggling for the security of a few sailors, whom, in the face of heaven and earth, they falsely call vagabonds from England, Ireland, and Scotland, whom our government is wickedly protecting at the hazard of the ruin of their country! Almighty father! To what an ebb is man capable of descending! Let us suppose for a moment that the illustrious Hull, Jones, Perry, Porter, Decatur, M'Donough, or any other of that constellation of heroes, who have bound their country's brows with a wreath of imperishable glory, had been pressed by a Cockburn, their proud spirits subjected to his tender mercies, and crushed by the galling chain and the rope's end! What a scene for a painter—what a subject for contemplation—what a neverdying disgrace to those whose counsels would persuade the nation to submit to such degradation!"[14]

Never, said Carey, was a war more justified. Our trade with fifty millions of the inhabitants of Europe was annihilated. In little more than a year, in 1803 and 1804, over twelve hundred seamen, claiming to be American citizens, sought the relief and protection of the American government thru the British government and the American agent. The self-respect

---

[12] *The Olive Branch,* p. 210.

[13] *Ibid.,* p. 213.

[14] *Ibid.,* p. 216.

and prestige of our nation must have been completely destroyed by further submission.

What was doubtless one of the most convincing and conciliating parts of *The Olive Branch* is the proof, thru the statistics supplied by the treasury reports, that the so-called "commercial states," the New England group, were really at this period of decidedly lesser importance as exporting, shipping, and importing states than those to the west and south of them. Their contention, then, that they were the great sufferers by the war thru the blow that it dealt at their commerce was greatly weakened.

That the book sketched in such limited space produced a wide and profound impression is beyond question. The number of editions testify to its popularity. At least eight issues were demanded—four from Carey's own press and one each at Boston, Middlebury, Vermont, Cincinnati, and Winchester, Virginia.

The second edition of one thousand copies was sold out in five weeks. Peace did not limit the demand, on the contrary it increased. As the New England states formed the section in which the work was most necessary, Carey attempted to get it printed in Boston. His offer of the free privilege of printing an edition there was accepted, and although the edition appeared after peace had been declared, it was immediately sold out. The fifth edition, also printed under gratuitous privileges, and issued at Middlebury, consisted of one thousand, nine hundred and twenty copies. When we consider that *The Olive Branch* was no mere pamphlet but a decidedly substantial octavo volume, we see that its utility must have been fully recognized. "No political work, to my knowledge," writes Carey, "has ever had an equal degree of success in America, except the 'Common Sense.' Four editions were sold in eight months; two more are at this moment in the press; and a seventh, as I said, is about to be printed. Nevertheless, it is not quite twelve months since the work was begun, and not ten since the first edition was published."[15]

[15] *The Olive Branch*, p. 32. The copy which I am using, and presumably the entire (sixth) edition, has pages 37 to 44 inclusive renumbered as pages 29 to 36. The reference is to the first page 32.

One need not go far afield to discover reasons why *The Olive Branch* was so popular. The subject was one of overwhelming importance. Too clearly could everyone see the imminent danger which threatened the Union, and tho there were politicians of influence and power who were willing to attain leadership thru the ruin of their country, however small the fraction of it which they led and however despicable the methods employed, yet the immense body of the people were patriotically alive to their danger and only seeking light and certainty in the midst of doubt and distraction. To such *The Olive Branch* must have been in the nature of a revelation. In its pages they found not the unsupported, exaggerated, and inflammatory excesses, which formed such a large part of the newspaper articles of the times and of the utterances from factional pulpit and platform, but calm and judicious statements backed by documents at whose authenticity and weight there could be no cavil. They must have felt, too, the essential fairness of the writer, extended even to his hereditary enemy, Great Britain. The free use of capitals and of italics, with the frequently admonishing index hand, made the work easy to read for even the most careless and unlearned. Carey was no mean master of argument, and many of his points must have gone home with decisive force. One rises from a perusal of *The Olive Branch* with the feeling that wide and accurate reading, a vigorous mind with special ability in polemics, absolute fairmindedness, and flaming patriotism have here united in the production of a work that falls little short of a classic of its kind.

It entitles Carey to a large space in any study of the development of American nationalism. As an impassioned plea for union and for resistance to the arrogance of Great Britain in the impressment of American citizens, it can hardly be read without a feeling of indignation for Great Britain and a blush of shame for a party so treacherous that it was willing to let its fellow countrymen meet the alternative of firing upon their flag or of facing the gallows or the hardly less horrible prison hulk. Poe calls it a " quixotic publication,"[16] but with com-

[16] Edgar Allen Poe, *The Southern Literary Messenger,* Richmond, Virginia, 1836, Vol. II, p. 203–5. Article reviewing Carey's *Autobiography.*

plimentary connotation, and if *Don Quixote* accelerated the downfall of a crumbling institution no less must *The Olive Branch* have caused many a potential overthrower of his own government to pause in his career.

The War of 1812 was in itself a powerful influence against the synchronous development of a national literature. The conditions that preceded it were also anything but favorable; for the long swell of the two titanic movements in Europe—the French Revolution, and especially the Napoleonic wars,—was always evident in America. When Ebeling disburdens himself in long letters about the horrors that were going on around him, when Cobbett writes of the movements in Great Britain that he fights so bitterly, both are addressing the representative of a country which was hesitating between England and France. What chance was there in these hours of indecision that a great literature should yet appear? When an Armada is darkening the shores such a literature may be blossoming, for in such a case there is no division; when a great cause is being lost there may be some appealing notes of a passionate regret, a *Conquered Banner,* that carries conviction to all hearts; but when sullen hatred and mutual distrust are predominant there can be no true literature. Mr. Whitcomb, in his *Chronological Outlines of American Literature,* found singularly few entries for this period; and we can hardly accuse him of being too rigid in his requirements. The political situation was too all-absorbing and too uncertain for much energy to be turned into literary channels.

The demand for books during the struggle was extremely small—smaller than might be expected, for, in striking contrast to the Revolution, there was almost nothing except the *Olive Branch* to inspirit those carrying on the war or to allay the feeling of party hatred. A typical letter from Richmond, Virginia, August 24, 1813, says, " Business is remarkably dull here at present. We can sell nothing but Military Books and among them Duane's Handbook for Infantry takes the lead— nearly all of those last sent me are already sold, and the demand is still great. It takes a long time to get a parcel of books bound here, for all the men are gone to the war." Only once is a mistake made. A shocked Quaker of New Jersey threatens to "dispatch" "20 copies of *Sword Exercise*" by putting them into a "good, large fire." Letters of agonizing doubt and fear containing no reference to books are frequent. Evidently the strong and helpful personality of Carey was clearly and widely recognized.

While the retarding forces of the War of 1812 upon the development of our literature have not been overestimated, there was another reason why the period was peculiarly barren. One race of literary men seemed to be dying out, and the new one which forms the pride of American literature was just coming into existence. Fessenden, last of the Hartford Wits, was to survive until 1837, but by 1812 the work of that group was almost over, as well as the work of those writers who made the literature of the Revolution. In 1812 when Joel Barlow and Joseph Dennie died, Harriet Beecher (Stowe) was six months old—names significant that

> The old order changeth, yielding place to new.

Two years before Charles Brockden Brown had died and Margaret Fuller (Ossoli) had been born. Soon Bryant, thru the *North American Review*, was to begin the prelude.

Deep as had been the humiliations connected with many of the features of the war and dire as the dangers had at times been, few wars have been equally well worth the winning; for if the war showed America that it must stand alone politically, no longer to be divided against itself in favor of France or of England, no less did it show those who had longingly turned their faces towards Great Britain as worthy alone of their intellectual homage, that America must seek her guidance from within. Soon all classes, feeling that they truly stood apart and must play their own game, had changed their attitude. William Henry Creagh writes from New York, May 6, 1818, "I commenced the publication of a weekly paper the 'European' for the purpose of giving the Political intelligence from the Old Country in *detail,* under the impression that the Natives of Great Britain and Ireland generally retained their ardour for the wellfare and interest of their Native Land after they had fixed their Abode in this Country, but I was so far mis-

taken that I find a general apathy pervades the greater part of
them, and instead of meeting with my anticipated success, I
have not sufficient subscribers to the work to pay my expenses."
Had the venture been made ten years earlier the result, in all
probability, would have been quite different.

The recovery of the demand for books was fairly rapid, that
for educational works especially so.[17] In some localities the
scarcity of money prevented large sales, the agents or dealers
frequently writing that the people want books but have no
money. A typical letter of the period is this one:

"AUGUSTA, GEORGIA January 24th 1817.
"*Dear Sir*
". . . Books of every description will sell well in this place.
Military works are in great demand, there is not one of any
kind for sale in Augusta. I can find immediate sale for 4
or 500$ worth of Modern Medical Publications; Law Books,
such as are suitable to American practice and of State publication are in demand. The following Books have been much
called for Peak's Evidence, Bell's Surgery, Ainsworth's Dictionary, Josephus' Works, Cicero Delphini, translated, Horace
Delphini do, Virgil, Main's Introduction, Pockett Testament,
do. Bibles, Davis' Sermons, Reading Exercises or sequel to
Mason's Spelling Book—Indeed everything suitable for a bookstore to vend, finds ready sale.
                              Yours etc. JAMES FINLATERS."

We have seen how American writers gained recognition in
Germany thru books of travel and other works of information.
There seems to be no evidence that American works, others
than those of this class, were read at all there during the first
quarter of the nineteenth century. But by the end of 1825
America had built up such a mass of literature and her younger
generation was showing such signs of literary ability that
England, was forced to take notice. The year before, John
Neal, who bubbled over with patriotism, had, after "appälling"
the American public by his genius as a novelist,[18] invaded the
enemies' country with a series of articles in *Blackwood's* on
American Writers, while on July 11, 1826, only six years after

[17] Several letters from Thomas Jefferson relating to such books occur about
this period. See Appendix V.
[18] See Appendix VI.

Sydney Smith's sneer, "Who reads an American Book?",
Miss Mitford writes to Haydon, apropos of *The Last of the
Mohicans* (which, be it observed, had just appeared that year),
"How wonderfully America is rising in the scale of intellect!
. . . If you have not read the American novels, do so. Depend
on it that America will succeed us as Rome did Athens;[19] and
it is a comfort to think that by their speaking the same beautiful language, Shakespeare and Milton will not be buried in
the dust of a scholar's library, but live and breathe in after
ages as they do now to us."[20]

In 1830 we find her engaged on the compilation of *Stories
of American Life by American Writers* which she prepares
from an immense mass of material. The work she thinks
"will be really very good—characteristic, national, various and
healthy."[21]

If it is now evident that American authors were able to get a
hearing in Great Britain,[22] no less evident was it that American publishers were becoming internationally prominent. In
1816 a London bookseller had written in response to Carey's
inquiry that "the 41st, Geo. III Cap. 107—prohibits the Importation of or selling of any Books reprinted from English
editions." Evidently American publishers were more than
meeting the domestic demand, and were beginning to seek new
territory. The law referred to seems to have been repealed,

[19] Compare Frederic Loliée, *A Short History of Comparative Literature*,
London, 1906, p. 297. M. Loliée thinks that, in the novel at least, the time
has already come.
[20] Rev. A. G. K. L'Estrange, *The Life of Mary Russel Mitford . . . Told
by Herself in Letters to Her Friends*. New York, 1870, Vol. II, p. 60.
[21] *Ibid.*, p. 111.
[22] Wiley & Putnam's *American Book Circular*, April, 1843, gives the following classification of American books printed in England.

Theology	68	History	22
Fiction	66	Poetry	12
Juvenile	56	Metaphysics	11
Travels	52	Philology	10
Education	41	Science	9
Biography	26	Law	9

Quoted in *Congressional Record*, Washington, 1888, Vol. XIX, p. 3237.

or else not enforced, for on May 18, 1823, Carey is able to write to his agent, Mr. John Miller of Henrietta Street, London, that "a very brisk trade is now carried on in the exportation of the works of Byron, Scott, Moore etc. etc. Several large editions have been recd from there lately, and as the American Editions are handsomely printed and at a low price they will be constantly in demand. They would form a very excellent medium of remittance for us if it could be done with profit and safety."

South America was also a field for American enterprise, tho many ventures here appear to have been unsuccessful. The first attempt was made at Buenos Ayres in 1821, but if we may judge from the absence of letters and orders, it soon proved a failure. A letter from Caracas, June 28 (received August 24), 1822, says that there is a good chance for a bookstore and for the sale of Spanish and French medical books especially. Apparently the Spanish colonists, who were winning their freedom at this period, sought inspiration in the heroes of the American Revolution; for this letter, as well as several later ones, contains a large order for framed engravings of American patriots. Spanish works on Masonry were also in active demand as the natives "are well disposed to initiate themselves in the Mysteries." A later order makes a special request for Spanish-English, English-Spanish and Spanish-French, French-Spanish grammars and for Spanish novels. A few days previously Carey had made arrangements for a representative at Gibraltar who should send him copies of any new Spanish work of interest that might be published, especially "Plays, Politics, Political Economy, etc." As only single copies for republication were desired it is evident that the books furnished South America were printed in this country and then forwarded, and that Carey was not merely a middleman between Spain and her colonies or former colonies. If any further evidence is needed it lies in the fact that the firm issued a Spanish dictionary in two volumes on October 22, 1822.

It seems best here, for chronological reasons, to take a brief survey of some of the activities of Carey as yet untouched upon and not immediately connected with the publishing trade;

for Carey the man is well worth more than a casual acquaintance.

The feeling of love for his mother country and of loyalty towards his people, the Irish, was never obscured in Carey by the strong sense of patriotism towards the United States. Ample testimony to this is shown in his constant aid to Irish immigrants, which is noticed elsewhere; and it has already been pointed out also how his injudicious and fervid defense of his country caused his banishment at an early age to France. It was this feeling which impelled Carey, in February, 1818, to undertake to defend Ireland and the Irish against the aspersions, " the unparalleled libels and calumnies," which had so long filled the pages of the English histories of Ireland, and especially those unjust accusations regarding the insurrection of 1641. Filled with a burning sense of indignation at the wrong done his countrymen, he had long planned such a work as his *Vindiciae Hibernicae*,[23] but the pressure of the daily affairs of a strikingly busy life had caused him to defer it, until in 1817 the deciding motive came in the publication of Godwin's *Mandeville* which revived many of the legends and horrors of the pretended massacre of 1641. Indignant at this perversion of the truth, and desirous to offset the wide effect of this pernicious romance, Carey began work in earnest upon the book that, next to *The Olive Branch,* is probably the most elaborate and sustained of his literary efforts. In addition to the incentive furnished by the romance, Carey had at this time another impelling reason for writing. The question of Catholic emancipation was then being discussed, and he felt that if he could only remove the great stumbling block, the tales of the plots and the massacre of 1641, he might give most potent aid in doing away with a situation in which the large majority of an unfortunate people was practically held in subjection by an inconsiderable minority.

[23] *Vindiciae Hibernicae: or Ireland Vindicated: An Attempt to Develop and Expose a few of the multifarious Errors and Falsehoods respecting Ireland in the Histories of May, Temple, Whitelock—and others, etc., Particularly in the Legendary Tales of the Conspiracy and Pretended Massacre of 1641.* Philadelphia, 1819. (Second edition, Philadelphia, 1823.)

Carey went into the matter of the preparation of the *Vindiciae* with great thoroughness. He purchased all the books that seemed to have any important bearing on the subject, bought a share in the New York Library, procured books from the Burlington Library, and borrowed everything available from his friends. Then he spent six months going through the books and liberally marking in parentheses the passages of importance. These passages he had copied by an amanuensis. The actual number of works quoted from is, in the second edition, seventy, and the number of separate quotations is eleven hundred and forty-three.

The methods employed remind one of Dickens during his most busy period, and they exceeded even Dickens' in the haste with which the copy was turned out and the pressure under which the work was performed. If Carey may be said to have been a genius at all, he was certainly what has been called a "large" and not a "fine" genius. Tho the following passage from the *Autobiography* (in the *New England Magazine,* Vol. VI, pp. 401–2) may be a somewhat extreme example of his method, it is worthy of quotation, for almost all Carey's writing were turned out at a pressure but slightly less than here described.

"As soon as I had twenty or twenty-five pages written, I put them into the hands of Mrs. Bailey, my printer, who every evening sent me a proof of the matter set up in type, and I returned the proof with a fresh supply of MS. next morning. The matter was printed in columns, and then arranged in proper order.

"Thus the MS. written one day was in type the next, throughout the whole progress of the work; and I was rarely ever more than one or two days ahead of the printer. I need not say how very disadvantageous was this plan. It fully accounts for the want of order and regularity in the work. . . .

"By a destitution in my cranium of the bump designating the power of arrangement, I have never been able to adjust my matter in proper order till it was set up in type, and a proof taken in columns, so that I might have a thorough view of the connection. Thus the paragraphs were so often transposed, that the first, and middle and last changed places. The sentences underwent the same changes,—some were wholly omitted,—some transposed,—others substituted,—and thus the whole appearance of the matter was altered. This system, the result of my utter deficiency of the proper mode of arranging my MS. had at all times greatly enhanced the expense of my printing."

The *Vindiciae,* he continues, cost $135 for corrections, and the setting up of the types but $369. And he adds, what soon becomes evident to his reader, that he was "at all times extravagant in the article of printing."

Carey felicitates himself upon the number of his quotations and the accuracy with which they are placed by page and by edition, so that refutation charges of unjust warping of an author's view would be impossible. To avoid any charges of partisanship he practically refrained from quoting from or referring to Catholic writers, but used Protestant authorities almost entirely. In these two features of his work Carey thinks that he stood much in advance of his times, and in an age when personal vituperation, misquotation, and flagrant partisanship was the rule, it seems that his view was justified.

The *Vindiciae Hibernicae* is occupied with the refutation of eight views of the Irish usually held, and supported by the majority of the British historians. It is not necessary here to enter into a discussion of each of these points. Two or three, however, upon which Carey throws most emphasis may be glanced at. He especially objects to the assertion that the Catholics of Ireland enjoyed full legal and social toleration in the exercise of their religion, and full protection in their property rights during the forty years preceding 1641. He traces the origin of the assertion that they did to Temple, and by aid of the "deadly parallel" he attempts to show that Clarendon, Warner, and Hume follow Temple. What is more important, however, than the fair case he makes for his side of the matter in this way are the extracts from state papers which he quotes in rebuttal of Temple and his imitators. These papers, which seem to have been overlooked or ignored by Temple, Clarendon, and the others go a long way towards proving the point which Carey is endeavoring to establish.

Turning then to another point which especially aroused his hatred of intolerance and injustice, Carey proceeds to prove that no real massacre ever took place or was planned in 1641.

The method used in this case is to point out the inconsistencies and absurdities in the narration of the occurrence as given in Temple's *History of the Irish Rebellion*. Temple's entire account, when clearly and coldly analyzed, as here by Carey, is absurd, and so Carey scores another point in his vindication. Most of the other historical authorities, he shows, have again followed Temple. The entire testimony upon which the large majority of the historians had founded their narrative is shown to rest upon hearsay, often thrice removed.

Of the *Vindiciae* Carey says in his *Autobiography* (in the *New England Magazine*, Vol. VII, p. 239) : " The publication of the Vindiciae Hibernicae was among the most important operations of my life—and one that affords me as much heartfelt satisfaction as anything I have ever done, not excepting the defense of the Protecting System, and the publication of the Olive Branch."

The entire work is worthy our notice as revealing once more the essential fairness and want of rancour of the man. The judicial cast of his mind comes out strongly. This is one of those books which shows his " Quixotic" nature in a most pleasing light. He undertakes the defense of an entire people, and attempts to change the verdict of the opinions of two other peoples (English and Americans) founded upon what had been received as history since Temple's *Introduction of 1695*.

A pamphlet of some interest related at many points to the *Vindiciae* was published at Philadelphia on January 1, 1829.[24] Perhaps it is enough to quote in part the descriptive title: *Letters on Religious Persecution, Proving, that the most Heinous of Crimes, has not been peculiar to Roman Catholics: But that when they had the Power, Protestants of almost every Denomination have been equally guilty . . . . In reply to a libellous attack on Roman Catholics, in an Address delivered to a Society of Irish Orange Men . . . By a Catholic Layman.* The entire pamphlet of sixty-eight quarto pages is a characteristic plea for toleration and mutual forgiveness of the crimes which Carey shows both Catholics and Protestants have committed against each other. Among those " liberal and superior spirits, who scorn to calumniate, abuse, and villify their un-

[24] The copy before me belongs to the fourth edition.

offending fellow citizens," to whom it is dedicated, there was none more liberal and just than the writer himself.

Although enough has already been said to bring out the fact that Carey had a rare spirit of love and helpfulness for his fellow-men, that fact has not received emphasis commensurate to its importance. It was not until his retirement from active business, in 1824, moreover, that this side of Carey's nature had full scope for its activity. Up almost to his death he was engaged by voice and by example in bettering the lot of his less fortunate fellow-men, tho his activities from 1824 to 1830 can be much more fully and accurately traced than from 1830 to his death, because of the greater amount of data obtainable on the former period.

In the first cessation from active business duties the mind of Carey appeared, as was quite natural in the new and strange leisure, to have gone back to the days of his youth and the scenes of Europe therein pictured. He was seized with a desire to alleviate transatlantic conditions. His warm sympathies had been previously aroused, however, in behalf of some of those Europeans, especially Irishmen, who had been bold or fortunate enough to reach this country. In 1792 he had called a meeting at the Philadelphia Coffee-House of a number of the most prominent Irishmen of the city to devise means for ameliorating the sufferings of the Irish immigrants who were then arriving in such large numbers, friendless and penniless. He had previously prepared a constitution for a society, which was read and adopted, and an organization called The Hibernian Society was formed for the relief of emigrants from Ireland. Hugh Holmes was elected president and Carey secretary, a position which he held for a number of years. In 1834 the society was still in existence with a long record of usefulness to its credit.

Now, however, in 1824, the sympathies of Carey had wider scope. He formed the design of encouraging, as far as he could, emigration from Europe that the condition of the masses might be bettered, for those who came, directly, and for those who stayed, indirectly, by the slight decrease in population. Perhaps this was one of those schemes which Poe had in mind when he said Carey was " Quixotic." At any rate Carey took himself seriously. In May, 1826, he published a pamphlet called *Reflections on the Subject of Emigration from Europe.* The *Reflections* was intended as a sort of handbook on the United States for the European. Carey endeavored to have it circulated as widely as possible in Europe, especially in Great Britain, in order that it might bring to the attention of the common people the advantages of the United States to those of unassured position in their own country. He designed it moreover as a warning to those in comfortable circumstances not to seek America as an El Dorado where a competency might become a fabulous fortune. America and Americans are discussed for the benefit of the foreigner. The independence of our citizens, the ease of acquiring landed property, the small burden of our taxation, and the freedom of religion are all entered into. In a love of parents for children and the mildness of discipline Carey finds matter for comment. He points out that primogeniture has not left its curse on the lives of the younger born. To the agricultural classes he extends a modified welcome, while the manufacturers are warned away. The mechanic is assured of ample employment.

The effect of Carey's pamphlet remains shrouded in obscurity. It may be deduced, however, that it gave no immediate aid to the Irish at least; for in July, 1828, Carey has another scheme again on foot for their relief. He thinks it possible to interest the employers of labor in sending an agent over to Ireland who should make clear to the inhabitants the manifold advantages of America and the means by which these blessings might be enjoyed. Those unable to pay for their own passage might be bound over for a period, as was often done at this time, to pay for their passage, but under strict watch to guard against this period being made too long. August 11, 1828, was appointed as the day for a meeting of all those interested. But alas! a little footnote records interest as a minus quantity.

If, however, the reader is inclined to smile at these two schemes of Carey, however much he may sympathize with the desire to aid humanity which prompted them, he can rest assured that fruit was not wanting to most of the labors of the formulator. For many years Carey had been actively engaged in charitable work in the city of Philadelphia, where the poor laboring women in particular recognized in him an unwearying friend. The ever-present denouncer of charity as an encouragement to idleness seems to have been particularly obnoxious in Philadelphia in 1829; for in March of that year Carey wrote an elaborate pamphlet entitled *Essays on the Public Charities of Philadelphia,* in which, to paraphrase the rest of the descriptive title, he vindicates the benevolent societies of the city from the charge of encouraging idleness, and places in strong relief the suffering and oppression under which labored the greater part of the women who depended on their industry for the support of themselves and their children.

This pamphlet, which Carey says cost him "more time, labour, and expense, than articles four times the size," reached at least five editions, the first three of which were printed and distributed gratuitously by the author, and the fourth of which was published partly at his expense. While not an advocate of woman's rights as now understood, his sympathies were actively aroused by the miserable compensation offered the woman who had to support herself, and perhaps a family. As the head of a committee he addressed a letter, January 13, 1829, to P. B. Porter, then Secretary of War, remonstrating with the government against the inadequate wages paid to women for making the governmental clothing for soldiers. Some correspondence ensued, but the government seemed disinclined to make a change. Carey draws a depressing picture of the misery and poverty in the Philadelphia of his day. He always combats the opinion, so prevalent among the rich, that the poor bring about their own evil condition thru idleness and mismanagement. Elsewhere he has an effective essay on the pernicious effect of continued, undeserved misfortune upon human character. The idea that such adversity is a good school for the great mass of humanity he shows is totally erroneous. Such vigorous attacks upon the accepted cant of his times show once more Carey's mental independence and clearness of vision.

"That the low rate of female wages—is discreditable to human nature—pernicious to the best interests of society—a fertile source of misery, immorality and profligacy—and loudly calls for a remedy "[25] is the theme he recurs to in forcible and at times eloquent terms. As one of a committee of seven he made a thorough investigation of the question, the results of which are embodied in his "Report on Female Wages," March 25, 1829. In the address "To the Ladies who have undertaken to establish a House of Industry in New York," May 11, 1830, he points out that the house, if it pay inadequate wages, would be almost a curse rather than a blessing. The "Address submitted for consideration to, and adopted by the Board of Managers of the Impartial Humane Society of Baltimore," May 15, 1830, is a contribution to the same subject. Is it not significant that organizations in these two cities should be seeking his aid? The Society for Bettering the Condition of the Poor was formed upon the plan Carey suggested, and began its work in Philadelphia on October 1, 1829. The influence Carey exerted in arousing the pity of the charitably inclined and in opening the eyes of the ignorant is not easily overestimated.

While Carey was thus engaged in relieving suffering at home, he had energy and sympathy enough to follow with deep attention a great drama then being enacted in southeastern Europe—the Greek Revolution. Edward Everett, the representative of Massachusetts in the lower house of Congress, writing from Washington, December 7, 1826, to Carey, at that time head of a committee formed for the relief of the Greeks, recommends that provisions be sent to the famine-stricken people then waging, against Turkey, a war for freedom that should have aroused the armed interference of Europe, but that seems to have excited small official attention

[25] *Public Charities in Philadelphia,* republished in *Miscellaneous Essays,* Philadelphia, 1830, p. 203. This volume (xii + 472, 8o) contains a wide variety of the essays of Carey, and is the best single publication for obtaining a glimpse of the multifold activities and catholic tastes of the author.

from any government. Four days after the receipt of this letter, Carey, as chairman, issued an eloquent appeal to the public "in the hope of awaking the slumbering sympathies of this great and rising empire in favor of one of the most interesting nations that ever existed—a nation whose struggles for everything dear and sacred to human nature, under almost every possible disadvantage, has never been exceeded, and but rarely equalled, for the most inflexible devotion to country, and the most heroic valour. The annals of the world, since ruthless warfare began to devour the human race, presents nothing of patriotism and bravery more honourable to our nature than the defense of Missolonghi."[26]

Since it seemed impossible to secure armed intervention by the government, Carey devoted all his energies to raising funds for the relief of the wounded and the helpless non-combatants. In *The Case of the Greeks,* he dwells upon the unhappy fate which awaits the helpless women when taken captive; he compares our Revolution with that which the Greeks were waging—the provocation to resistance so infinitely less, the aid afforded the Greeks so strikingly in contrast to that we received, and the results of a failure so appallingly more tragic. One of his most eloquent appeals was issued without the knowledge of the committee. Of this action Carey writes a defense characteristically free and determined.

"If, however, 'offences must come,' in the discharge of duty, I cannot, will not shrink from its performance on that account. I unhesitatingly steered that course at an earlier period of life, when I held my fortunes and the support of a numerous family by the very frail tenure of public opinion, almost as fickle as the wind itself; and it would be extraordinary and inconsistent, indeed, to change the system, in my present circumstances, with little to hope or fear from mankind—and having, moreover, arrived at that advanced stage of existence, which nearly touches the goal which separates time from eternity."[27]

Other activities of Carey which show him more or less as a philanthropist may be briefly noticed here. In January, 1827,

[26] *The Case of the Greeks,* in *Miscellaneous Essays,* p. 298.
[27] *Ibid.,* p. 305–6.

he tried to secure a change in the system whereby regiments of artillery were periodically shifted from one part of the country to another. The next year he addressed a strong appeal to Congress to pension the needy soldiers—especially the officers—of the Revolution, or to make them some financial remuneration for losses which many of them had incurred. He attacked the race question in September, 1829.[28] Arguing from statistics, he showed that by the year 1870 the negroes in many of the southern states would exceed the number of whites, a truly appalling condition, he thinks. Some two years before, Carey had written two pamphlets[29] on emancipation, in which, however, he arrived at no very definite conclusions. Forcible emancipation seemed to him too absurd to be discussed. He turned then later to Liberia, involved in formidable difficulties tho it was, as the solution of the problem.

In 1827 Carey was led to advocate the establishment of infant schools or kindergartens, rather as a philanthropic work than as an educational venture. Such schools, by relieving the working woman from household cares, would, his idea was, enable her to work more effectively for support. One other item which should not be omitted is that Carey in 1796 established the first Sunday-school society.

[28] *African Colonization*, in *Miscellaneous Essays*, pp. 214–18.
[29] *Emancipation of the Slaves in the United States*, in *Miscellaneous Essays*, pp. 222–32.

CHAPTER V

THE STRUGGLE OF AMERICAN LITERATURE AGAINST THE EXPLOITATION OF FOREIGN AUTHORS BY AMERICAN PUBLISHERS

"LONGMAN & Co. April 15th, 1817.

" . . . We are very desirous to make some arrangement by which we should receive such new works that come out as may be likely to bear publication in this Country. If you can make any such arrangements for us we will allow Two hundred & fifty dollars per annum, provided the person will forward them per first vessel from London or Liverpool in order that we may receive them first. . . . Our booksellers are so very active that it would require very considerable attention to forward them by first and fastest sailing vessels. We should wish to receive every new work of popularity and particularly those of Miss Porter, Lord Byron, Miss Edgeworth, W. Scott, Leigh Hunt, Author of Waverley, Moore, Miss Burney, Mrs. Taylor, Lady Morgan, Dugald Stuart, etc., etc. We are particularly desirous to receive McIntosh's Great Britain, Vol. I as soon as out. In short we should wish the person who might undertake it, to use his judgment in selecting for us every work at all likely to bear republication—New Voyages and Travels of merit are also requested."

The significance of the paragraph quoted above is not easily overestimated; for if it be the first of its character, and, so far as I can find, it is, it indicates the genesis of an influence that was to contribute very largely to the development of the short story in America, to the obscuration of the American playwright for almost three-quarters of a century, to the rise of the American magazine, and to the struggle of the American novelist against strong odds until 1891. The present study is necessarily but a sketch of the beginnings of that influence.

We have seen in Chapter IV that an exchange with Germany was formed as early as 1793, but it was largely barren in its results. American authors had little to fear from direct

German competition, but they did have much to fear from German literature in an English dress. Mr. Wilkins, in his admirable monograph, *German Literature in America* (1762–1827), has found one hundred and eighty-seven issues of German productions from American presses; but a glance at his list shows that fully nine-tenth are printed from English translations. It is to be noted, however, that few were printed more than once, and very probably the editions were small. There were six editions of *The Sorrows of Werther,* it is true, but compared with its severity in Europe our attack of Werther-fever was slight indeed. Kotzebue, moreover, whose name occurs by far the most often, appealed to only a limited class —the lovers of the drama—and possibly some of the editions were printed for stage use only. The competitive effect of Spanish literature was almost non-existent. That of France directly was very small, altho, especially at a later period, it became very powerful thru English translations; for no history of the American theater will be at all complete without a consideration of French plays that gained a hearing in America with the English stage as a popularizing intermediary. The still later popularity of the French novel is of course beyond the limits of this discussion. But with English literature of every sort at hand, there was no need of a benumbing translation or of adaptation from that of another race.

Before the appearance of Miss Porter's *Scottish Chiefs* there was, as already noticed, a very considerable business of reproducing English classics, which reached this country thru the ordinary course of travel or importation. No one thought of objecting to these or attempting to exploit them any more than a modern publisher would attempt to exploit *Robinson Crusoe.* The demand for such books, while steady, was limited; and when a copy of a new book was brought over there were not a dozen publishers ready to bid for it and rush an edition thru the press in thirty-six hours. But when, even as early as 1811, a dealer at Pittsburg can write in the familiar phrase, " new novels are all the rage here now," a new and disastrous influence must be taken into consideration; for it was English novels—those of Miss Edgeworth and Miss Porter—to

which he referred. Seven years later a Philadelphia correspondent of Maria Edgeworth could write, "'Waverley,'
'Guy Mannering,' etc., have excited as much enthusiasm in
America as in Europe. Boats are now actually on the lookout
for 'Rob Roy,' all here are so impatient to get the first sight
of it."[1] In 1820 not a single copy of *Ivanhoe* could be procured for Colonel Campbell[2] in all Philadelphia; tho doubtless the Colonel had only to wait a few days for another huge
edition.

It will be recalled that Mrs. Radcliffe and her school were
very popular in America, but the period of Mrs. Radcliffe's
activity, 1789–1797, did not coincide with that of any American novelist, or at least retard it. Indeed the effect on Brown
and, later, on Neal was no doubt beneficial in a positive way,
in inspiring them to write; just as Cooper was negatively inspired. When however the last two were involved in the
formidable competition of the early twenties the effect was
anything but helpful; and on men of unestablished reputations
and of lesser genius it must in many cases have been stifling.
A glance at English literature at about the time when Neal,
Cooper, Miss Sedgwick, Simms, and others were making their
first appearance before the American public, and Irving had
begun to produce with some regularity, shows that the field
was occupied by Miss Porter, Miss Edgeworth, Miss Austen,
and Scott. Miss Porter, it might be objected, had published
nothing very popular since *The Scottish Chiefs* (1810); but
the immense and enduring vogue of that novel alone necessi-
tates that she be taken into account, while the number of calls
for *The Mysteries of Udolpho* and Mrs. Roche's *Children of
the Abbey*, which I should be inclined to regard as the most

---

[1] Grace A. Oliver, *A Study of Maria Edgeworth*, Boston, 1882, p. 315.

[2] This was in all probability Colonel Robert Campbell (1775–1831) who
was born in Augusta County, Virginia, and served under Christian against
the Cherokees and at the battle of King's Mountain. He was for many
years colonel of a regiment and for forty years magistrate of Washington
County, Virginia. His manuscript diary is interesting to the close student
of the period, while his account of the battle of King's Mountain (published
in the Holston *Intelligencer* in October, 1810) is much quoted in Draper's
King's Mountain and its Heroes.

popular British novel in America before Scott, tho diminishing was yet large. Against Scott we must match Cooper, if we can. Is it possible to say for a moment that the other three American novelists should, and did, have the weight with the reading public that the three English writers had?

In poetry, other than dramatic, the competition of the republications did not have a very deterrent effect. In the first place poetry was not read so much in America from 1787 to 1823 as literary historians are inclined to believe. The number of old copies of poetical works surviving from this period seems to have unduly impressed them, while the scarcity of novels has too often been accounted for upon the hypothesis that they had little vogue. But when we reflect that even now beautiful presentation copies of poems lie for months on our tables without the symmetry of their outlines being marred, while the family and their friends have dog-eared the latest novel in two weeks, we may be sure that the novel of one hundred years ago was often worn out and went to kindle the fire, while the poem was preserved for posterity. November 6, 1818, Carey writes to Philip Freneau that the last edition of his poems, which consisted of only 1000 copies, was about exhausted after nine years. "The demand here has ceased." Doubtless other publishers were writing similar letters. An example, taken at random, of the amount of poetry the people were actually demanding about 1812, may be found in an order from Reading, Pennsylvania, October 17, 1812: Out of eighty-one titles, four belong to poetry: 1 *Goldsmith's and Collins' Poems* ($0.75); 1 *Marmion* ($1.25); 1 *Lay of the Last Minstrel* ($1.00); 1 *Lady of the Lake* ($1.00). The total amounts to $188.60. The proportion holds thru hundreds of bills of a representative dealer whose business was too general and too extended merely to reflect any one class or any one section. Before Mrs. Radcliffe, the proportion of poetry is a little larger. (*Ossian's Poems,* it might be noticed, have a large run as late as 1800); in 1823, it is smaller. It is, however, to the credit of America that the *Lyrical Ballads,* which at first fell dead in England, were republished, in 1802, in Philadelphia, and became immediately popular. But it would be hardly possible to flood the market with poetry. A Neal[3] or a Dumas may furnish reading for a lifetime, but even a Lope de Vega has his limits.[4]

As observed above, our earliest novelist of genius suffered little from the competition of his British contemporaries. The reasons are apparent. The eighteenth century English classics so often republished lacked the popular appeal of newness, and while the demand was steady it was not monopolistic. American publishers were in Brown's time not quite numerous enough even fully to supply the market without importing, so that competition between them was never serious. The last and most important reason is to be found in the limited amount of fiction which was then being produced in England. Brown's productive period as a novelist, it will be remembered, ended in 1801. By this date Mrs. Radcliffe, Mrs. Roche, and Monk Lewis were in the field (Miss Edgeworth was not popular till

---

[3] " He boasted that within twelve years he had written enough to fill fifty-five duodecimo volumes." William P. Trent, *A History of American Literature*, New York, 1903, p. 251.

[4] Not only was Freneau neglected at this period but our first authentic poet, Byrant himself, was slow to obtain an audience. " Of the 1821 edition of his poems," writes Mr. Sturges, " 750 copies were printed and only 270 sold; a profit of $15.00, minus eight cents, for five years' sale." (*The Poetical Works of William Cullen Bryant*, New York, 1908, p. xlvi.) The contents of this volume should have indicated to every true lover of poetry that no mere rhymster was among them, for it included among others, " The Ages," " To a Waterfowl," " The Yellow Violet," " Green River," and " Thanatopsis." It is not until eleven years later (1832) that Bryant undertakes another volume, and practically all, if not all, the poems included in this edition had been tested through the medium of the magazines. It is interesting to note in connection with this volume that it is only through the good offices of Irving who " edits " it that Bryant secures its publication in London, and then only by an obscure publisher. (*Ibid.*, pp. xxiii–xxiv.) The popularity of Trumbull's *McFingal* (1776–84) is well established. This may be accounted for, in part, not by a love of poetry *per se*, but by its peculiarly opportune appeal to the revolutionary spirit of the times. Were more copies of Butler the poet sold than of Butler the Cavalier; of Trumbull the poet than of Trumbull the revolutionist; of Bryant the poet than of Bryant the publicist? Another fairly well read poet of this period is Joel Barlow, whose *Vision of Columbus* had readers estimated at about five thousand, American, British, and French—surely no enormous popularity. The vogue of the poetic classics of Great Britain has already been touched upon at page 31.

much later). Lewis, it seems, was not widely read. Mrs. Radcliffe had achieved great popularity thru the *Mysteries of
Udolpho;* but while there was some demand for the *Sicilian
Romance* and *The Romance of the Forest,* it was never very
great, and the average reader then, as now, was no doubt
inclined to regard her as largely a writer of one work. Mrs.
Roche was eminently so. In the limited output of these writers
lay the salvation of the American novelist of that time. When
Scott appeared one immensely popular novel followed another
in quick succession. The American public after devouring the
latest looked eagerly for the next. Hardly had Scott ceased to
produce when Dickens, ably seconded by Marryat, began a
series equally popular; and, when Marryat fell out, Benjamin
Disraeli was ready to fill the gap. From Waverley in 1814, to
The Mystery of Edwin Drood, 1870, the year that did not
produce at least one highly popular British novel was a barren
period. Against this continuous stream the American novelist
was compelled to wage a bitter struggle.

It was probably the popularity of Miss Edgeworth's novels
that first caused our publishers to see the possibilities of the
exploitation of British authors, but not until Scott appeared
was it systematically done. The letter quoted at the beginning
of the chapter seems to have been the first step in the movement; but other publishers were soon in the field, and by about
1820 the competition between them was as keen as anything
in modern business life, and the happy, golden age described[5]
by Noah Webster in 1791 was over. Longman & Company
referred the letter to Mr. John Miller of Henrietta Street, a
dealer, and publisher in a small way, who until 1861, represented Lea & Blanchard, successors, thru several firms, of
Mathew Carey. A few of the other largest American firms
also secured agents.

The intensity of the competition and the methods of meeting
it may be judged by the following letter.

" Mr. John Miller, June 17th, 1823.

" We have rec'd ' Quentin Durward ' most handsomely and

[5] See Appendix VII. The book in question is Webster's *Grammatical
Institute,* which included his truly remarkably popular *Speller.*

have the Game completely in our own hands this time. In 28 hours after receiving it, we had 1500 copies sent off or ready to go, and the whole Edition is now nearly distributed. In two days we shall publish it here and in New York and the Pirates may print it as soon as they please. The opposition Edition will be out in about 48 hours after they have one of our Copies but we shall have complete and entire possession of every market in the Country for a short time. Independently of profit, it is in the highest degree gratifying to be able to manage the matter in our own way without fear of interference. When we rec'd the Vol. wanting the few last pages, we were vexed to think that a long passage might keep us out of them so long that we might lose all the advantage already gained, but the Mail of next morning put us in the best of humor by bringing the remaining pages. Could not Messrs. Constable & Co. furnish us a manuscript Copy of the last few pages, so as not to be obliged to wait until the whole is at press? It frequently happens that we are 70 or 80 days without intelligence from England. One day will bring a vessel in 60 days, next day in 50 and the following day one in 40 or 35 so that our 15 or 20 days are completely lost to us. We are very desirous of taking every precaution against losing the advantage for which we pay so heavily, and which is lost unless we have a few days start as we cannot bring the book into the Market so soon as the opposition. They publish as soon as they can have ten Copies from the press while we cannot until we have at least 2000 or 2500. They print for their own stores. We do it for the supply of a whole country, and we must send off to our correspondents as soon as we publish here. You will please to take all these matters into consideration and make the best arrangements in your power for us. The transmission of the sheets direct from Edinburg to Liverpool is a great improvement as it must save much time. In future request C. &. Co. to make the Bundles as before requested. Part 1. No 1, 2 and 3 and so on in order to prevent a repetition of the former unlucky blunder. We regret that you must have been put to inconvenience from the delay of remittances but the work came out so rapidly that it was impossible for us to place funds there in time. In general at least three or four months elapse between the receipt of the first and last parts thus affording time to remit after leaving off the work. Could you not arrange with them to pay in 60 days after the work is completed? You would thus be certain of having money in time. You may rely upon having the Amt. always in future as soon as we are advised that we are to have the work. We hope soon to hear from you with the 1st Vol. of the next work."

Signs of really acute competition for the latest English novel first begin to appear in the early part of 1820. In that year Wells & Lilly of Boston insert their name as joint publishers with Carey & Son of *Ivanhoe,* tho it appears they did not have a single copy in print. Calls for immediate orders of *The Monastery* appear. On October 9, L. & F. Lockwood of New York write:

"We should feel it a great favor if you would send us of the *first* going off *Fifty copies* at least of the Abbott. Would it not be well to delay the publication for a day or two so that they may come together, as the Printers here stand ready to lay hold of the first copy you send.

"Having been disappointed in the Monastery we beg you to give us a fair chance this time."

When we reflect that all three of these novels were first published in 1820, their vogue and the activity of the publishers become apparent. On August 14, 1821, Wells & Lilly complain that Carey & Son are printing Lady Morgan's *Italy* after they had said that they would not do so. Van Winkle of New York, they continue, is also issuing an edition. Miller felicitates himself in 1822 that he has at least three days start of the other American agents in forwarding a copy of Horace Walpole's *Memoirs of the last ten years of George the Second.* On February 5, 1822 Carey & Sons write to the Secretary of the Treasury, complaining that it takes too long for new books to get thru the Custom House at New York, where they are shipped because there are more vessels entering at that port; and that they are thus delayed in getting to press. It is, they write, a very serious matter to lose merely the time necessary for the printers' copy to come from New York and the finished edition to be returned there, for in that short interval some other vessel might bring a copy. Here we have in a few lines a powerful factor in the rising supremacy of New York as a publishing center, at this time[6] the equal of Philadelphia, soon to outstrip it. Ten days after the last letter, Collins & Co.

[6] It is obviously impossible to fix any definite date. Some authorities place it as early as 1810. To the enterprise and aggressiveness of Harper & Brothers, who became prominent about 1817, more than to any other firm is the result due. The year 1810 seems entirely too early.

reply to a protest: "We believe it has been the uniform practice both here and in Boston to print in each place editions of Scott's novels as soon as received, on the ground that the demand was so great that it might be done without infringing the customary rights in such cases." On July 14, 1822, Carey & Sons write to Miller, "We have now 9 printing offices employed to get it (*Fortunes of Nigel*) out by to-morrow, Saturday, morning, and an Edit. is printing in New York to be published on Monday." In 1825 Carey & Lea received advance copies of the eleventh, twelfth and thirteenth cantos of *Don Juan.* It was immediately given out to about thirty compositors, and in thirty-six hours an American edition was on sale. Indeed so intense became the desire to be the first to get copies of Scott's novels for reprinting that it appears that some one (not necessarily an American) stole the "first copies of the Waverley novels" from the office of Constable and Company.[7] They accused Carey & Sons, but withdrew the charge in the next letter.

Such details might be accumulated for pages. Nor need it be thought that American publishers alone were eager to exploit the work of others: the crime was world wide. Ebeling, as already noticed, had written in 1793 that unauthorized translations would undersell American imports in Germany. John Souter, No. 73, St. Paul's Churchyard, was agent for American publications in England, Ireland, and Scotland; Miller was, in addition to acting as agent for Carey, also on the lookout for American works to republish himself or to sell to others. "I am reprinting," he writes on October 30, 1822, "the New England Tale and expect good sales for it; Murray reprints the Pioneers."[8] *The Pioneers* was first published in America on February 1, 1823, so that it seems to have been first issued in England.[9] Other works of Cooper appeared in England in

[7] See Appendix VIII.

[8] Campbell, according to this letter from Miller, expressed to him a desire to have his own biography, which was then in preparation, first published in America.

[9] *The Pioneers* was to have been brought out as early as the fall of 1822, but the yellow fever epidemic that summer paralyzed the printing business in New York. Extracts had been previously published in newspapers, and

the same year as in America, as did also those of Irving; and they may have been issued there first,[10] for so bad were conditions that American authors were often forced to adopt this course.[11]

The effect of such competition upon publishers as well as authors, both British and American, was disastrous, especially so upon American publishers. The publication of popular works from across the ocean became a gamble in which the winnings went to the largest and best organized firm—when the wind and waves favored. The smaller firms suffered morally as well as financially: morally in that they so often succumbed to the temptation to republish works to which some other publisher had obtained a moral, tho not a legal, right by a partially adequate payment to the foreign proprietor; financially, because if they refused to offer the "best seller" many of their customers ceased to patronize them. For a firm at Boston, let us say, to order from Philadelphia would not answer, for twelve days were thus lost. Publishers, even the largest, must quite frequently have found that an edition of some work only fairly popular, issued a little too late, must be put upon an already glutted market. Works of special nature were therefore seldom reprinted, for the financial loss in case of a rival edition was very serious. Distrust and jealousy sprang up on every side. Such conditions prevalent in America must have been in a lesser measure reflected in England.

The effect upon American authors was unfortunate in the extreme. None of them, not even Irving and Cooper, was ever so popular for a continuous period as Scott, Byron and Dickens; so that had it been possible to sell their books at the same price the sales would have been smaller. But the neces-

the book was awaited with great impatience. By noon on Februrary 1, 3500 copies had been sold. (Thomas R. Lounsbury, *James Fenimore Cooper*, Boston, 1883, pp. 40–41.) Compare also Bryant page 83, note.

[10] "Authors of established reputation" writes Mr. Henry C. Lea, "who could arrange in advance with English publishers would do it so as to obtain copyright by first publication there."

[11] "Address of certain authors of Great Britain to the House of Representatives of the United States, in Congress assembled." Reprinted in *The Congressional Record*, Washington 1888, Vol. XIX, p. 3241.

sity of paying the author a fair royalty or of buying his copyright made the price of his works considerably higher than those of the British writer to whom no adequate returns could be made by the most conscientious publisher, because any amount advanced secured merely a few hours' start of the pirates and the goodwill of a limited number of the public. The latter often refused to pay a high price for even the American book that they knew to be good, when they could secure cheaper a popular English book. As a result, the sales of American works and the profits of the writer were appreciably decreased. Irving still further embarrassed his publishers by continually demanding fine editions. In the case of an author who, like Cooper, made many failures, the public often hesitated to buy and the publishers to publish. The $2,600 which the firm inform Cooper, November 12, 1836, they have lost on *The Monikins* was, however, no doubt repaid several times over by *Pickwick Papers* and *Sketches by Boz,* which had also first appeared in 1836.[12] Of *Mercedes of Castile* (1840) only 1700 copies out of 4000 had sold by February 10, 1841. The publishers suggest that the author should remit a portion of the copy money, " owing to the fact that we stated to you our disappointment in the character of the work before publication, it being different to what you stated previously to finishing it." The reply seems to have been cutting. Few but the largest firms could allow personal friendship or patriotism to influence them in the slightest degree.

The immediate price of American books was decreased, but without proportionately increasing the sales.

" J. FENIMORE COOPER, Esq. Nov. 13, 1834.

" . . . We wish you to remark that we have been *compelled* to sell Books cheaper than we did formerly. When your early works were published, English novels retailed for $1.50 and American could be sold at $2. Now the other retails at $1. and the other at about $1.50 or less. It is true that the nominal wholesale price is still $1.50, but it is necessary to make discounts from that price in proportion to the quantity purchased. We cannot estimate the product at more than $1.30 per copy."

[12] The rival firm of Carey and Hart published Bulwer's *Rienzi* and Marryat's *Mr. Midshipman Easy* in the same year.

Meanwhile other prominent Americans were having their troubles also. In 1836 Irving was offered $4000 for the right of printing 5000 copies of *Astoria,* but he was refused the fine edition upon which his heart was set.[13]

In 1841 and 1842 a severe business depression marked by the failure of the United States Bank, by the refusal of Pennsylvania and Maryland to pay interest due on their state debts, and by Dorr's Rebellion, swept over the country. Typical of this period are the following letters:

"Washington Irving Esq   March 2 1841.

"We have yours of the 25th ulto. in relation to the volume you are preparing.[14] The times are most sadly against the publication of any work requiring even a fair ed.

"We are issuing chiefly to keep ourselves before the world & few books we now print exceed 500 copies for an edition. We shd be pleased to give the volume to the public. The great quantities however that formerly sold when the South & S. West were opened, cannot now be managed. Never the less we think we can sell as many as any other house & the best shall be done. There must be something very attractive in the life of a girl of sixteen that could move you, & we shd rely more on your own opinion of the work than what we can now suppose would be attractive to the many, in one who died

---

[13] Irving seems to have been rather indolent as well as a lover of fine things; for *Mahomet,* which he had promised for 1839, was not published until 1850; tho his publishers repeatedly urge him to get it ready as soon as possible. *Tales,* promised in 1842, is probably *Wolfert's Roost,* 1855.

[14] The volume in question is the *Poetic Remains* of Margaret Miller Davidson (Mar. 26, 1823–Nov. 25, 1838) which the firm (Lea & Blanchard) published in 1841. Miss Davidson passed an early childhood of remarkable promise. When hardly more than six years of age she wrote in two days, *The Tragedy of Alethia. Lenore,* the longest of her poems, contains passages of considerable beauty. Her numerous shorter poems are instinct with a devotional ardour of rare quality. The poems of her scarcely less gifted sister (Lucretia Maria Davidson 1808–1825) seem to have been included in this volume, which had a biography of the younger sister by Irving. Miss Sedgwick wrote a memoir of the elder sister which appeared in Sparks' *American Biography.* The poems of both sisters were published in one volume (*Poetical Remains*) at Boston in 1859. *Amir Khan and other Poems* by Lucretia Maria Davidson, published, with a sketch of her life by S. F. B. Morse, in 1829, is the "volume of poems" alluded to just below. Both sisters were indeed in their rare promise "of those that died before the dawn."

so young. A volume of Poems by her sister was published some time since but its sale was not we believe very extensive. All this however, is not to the point.

"We think it would be better to print an edition of 2500 copies for a first ed for which we could allow twenty two cents per copy payable at 9 mos from publication & if it was sufficiently attractive could be stereotyped or set up again for 2000 copies at same price per copy. Would this not be your best course? It may be that the work may prove more attractive than we suppose & many thousands may be wanted. We would of course push it with our best efforts.

"You may remember that you had 30 cts for the Crayon Miscellany, but you stereotyped that. In the present case you require the composition to be paged by us, on the 2500 which would be about the difference. There is another consideration —we now give larger discounts to the trade than we did then.

"You will we think agree with us about the number of copies proposed to be first printed when we inform you that the first sale of vol 3 Crayon Miscellany did not exceed 2500 copies.

"Pray give our views of the matter your consideration & let us have the pleasure of hearing soon from you."

"WASHINGTON IRVING Esq   Mar 3 1842

"Yours of the 26th inst. did not reach us until the evening of the 1st inst. We have given much consideration to the matter and have to say that It would give us great pleasure to be able to meet your wishes at once, but the country is in such a condition, that we wld not be justified now in making such an operation as you propose. In the present and paralyzed state of the currency, we do not believe that a new & necessarily expensive edition would be successful. It would require a very large expenditure & consequently large receipts—the latter could scarcely be hoped for in the present distressed state of almost every portion of the country. Hereafter it may answer.

"For the present we should prefer to continue our arrangement for two years at one thousand dollars per annum & include the right to publish Astoria, Miscellany, etc in it, Or if you wish to publish 'Mahomet' this spring & the two volumes of Tales, mentioned in your letter, to follow by June or July— these might be included in the two years right with the others, say the whole for five thousand dollars for the two years commencing at the time of publication of the last—we to reserve the right at the end of that period to publish a new edition of your works as you propose with the other vols selected, say for five or more years at the price of $2500 per annum. . . ."

Far more serious was the lot of Poe during this period of intense business depression.

"EDGAR A. POE, Aug. 16, 1841.

"We have yrs of the 13th inst. in which you are kind enough to offer us a 'new collection of prose Tales.'

"In answer we very much regret to say that the state of affairs is such as to give very little encouragement to new undertakings. As yet we have not got through the edition of the other work and up to this time it has not returned to us the expense of its publication. We assure you that we regret this on your account as well as our own—as it would give us great pleasure to promote your views in relation to publication."[15]

Tales of the Grotesque and Arabesque (1839)[16] is the "other work." The Prose Romances of Edgar A. Poe ("The Murders in the Rue Morgue," and "The Man that was Used up") was published at Philadelphia in 1843. In 1845 Wiley and Putnam of New York issued Tales by Edgar A. Poe. It seems impossible to determine which one of these, if either, is the "new collection." In any case, owing to the English reprint, Poe was not receiving any adequate returns for his work; and it may be that such a refusal to publish his tales had a worse effect upon his sensitive nature than the loss of the money they might have brought.

Four months later another genius receives bad news:

[15] This letter has been published by George E. Woodberry in his Edgar Allen Poe, Boston, 1885, p. 165. A previous letter to Poe (not found, see Woodberry, p. 164) had given the title as follows "some such title as this: —The Prose Tales of Edgar A. Poe, including 'The Murders in the Rue Morgue,' the 'Descent into the Maelstrom,' and all his later pieces, with a second edition of the Tales of the Grotesque and the Arabesque.

"The later pieces will be eight in number, making the entire collection thirty-three which would occupy two thick volumes." All profits were to go to the firm (as allowed before 1839 on Tales) and twenty copies only were to be given to Poe. When the work was nearly ready, he tried to get better terms, but the firm (Lea and Blanchard) refused and asked him to secure another publisher. (Ibid., pp. 116–17.) The work was published in two volumes in 1839 or 1840.

[16] Harrison (The Complete Works of Edgar Allan Poe, New York, 1902, Vol. xvi, p. 364) says 1840. The edition printed of the Tales of the Grotesque and Arabesque consisted of 750 copies only, says Mr. Henry C. Lea.

"Mr. W. Gilmore Simms, Dec. 16, 1841.

"'Confession' is a total failure, the 'Kinsman' will do better. We do not see much hope in the future for the American writer in light literature—as a matter of profit it might be abandoned.

"The channel seems to be glutted with periodical literature particularly the mammoth Weeklies—besides which we go into market for $1.50 a copy agt English reprints at 90c." . . .

Simms seems not to have followed the advice, tho possibly it had something to do with the researches in biography that punctuate the long series of novels that follow. Irving, Cooper, Poe, Simms,—if these four men were so harassed and, in one case at least, forced from the market, what must have happened to the writer of ordinary talents?

If the effect of competition on American authors was so dire it was also not inconsiderable on those of Great Britain—not so much by direct competition, for Irving and Cooper were the only Americans continuously read at this period, but by the indirect loss of profit and by the annoyance caused by garbled versions. Mrs. Radcliffe probably received nothing for her works. It has been conjectured that Scott's life would have been prolonged had an international copyright prevailed, so that full returns could have been made for works published in America.[17] The conscientious American publisher soon became accustomed to gauging values. Miller is instructed, in 1836, that except James, D'Israeli, Miss Edgeworth, and Marryat, with whom special terms must be made, no one will bear over five pounds. Lady Morgan, Hook, Mrs. Hall, Chamier, Horace Smith, Hood, the Author of Godolphin, Trevelyan, Grattan and the Countess of Blessington would bear that sum but not over it. In 1834 Miller is to offer Miss Edgeworth £25 to £40 for *Taking for Granted* (evidently *Helen*); in 1836, Bulwer £125 (but there was trouble brewing between Bulwer

[17] See "Address of certain authors of Great Britain to the House of Representatives of the United States, in Congress Assembled." Reprinted in *Congressional Record*, Washington, 1888, Vol. XIX, p. 3241. One likes to think in this connection of the struggling and yet unrecognized Carlyle as aided by Emerson, who undertook the publication, at his own risk, of *Sartor Resartus* and sent the proceeds to the author.

and Harpers), and James £50 to £60 for their next work. Four years later Dickens commands £150 to £225. Irving, we have noticed, is offered in 1842 $2500 per annum for the right of publishing his collected works for the next five years. By that year he has written twelve of his seventeen works.

In 1837 Carey & Co. had explained to Dickens why they could not afford to give more for his works, which naturally were not then worth so much as later.

" MR. SAML. DICKENS, June 14, 1837.

" On the first appearance of the Pick Wick Papers we undertook their publication in this country and have to this time pubd. 12 parts.

" Ere this you would have heard from us but this work with others had to succumb with the times[18] and it was doubtful if we would have been paid for more had we published them. But we conclude to venture to press with a volume or so and shall continue the papers.

" Under the hope that business will improve and the sales of the work extend, we have thought of the author and have requested our agent, Mr. John Miller, to furnish you with a draft on W. & I. Brown & Co., Liverpool, for £25 at 4 mos. which we beg you will accept not as a compensation, but as a memento of the fact that unsolicited a bookseller has sent an author, if not money, at least a fair representative of it. The amt. is small, and you can well understand why it is not more when we state that we shall sell the whole 12 pts., done up in 3 vols., to the trade for about five shillings net: After paying the cost of making this does not leave much for the Bookseller or Author. The novels that are published in England in 3 vols. are here printed in two and sold to the Trade for Three shillings per copy and the edition of 1000 copies, say such as Jack Brag, Rory O'More[19] etc. at such prices but little is made of them and it is but seldom that they will admit of any payment to authors, occasionally when a *first edition* will admit of a large impression this can be done but exceptions to that quantity are few.

[18] It may not be amiss to refer to the panic of this year, the Panic of 1837, which was caused by over speculation in land and by the wild cat banks, banks organized in the various parts of the country, and especially in the Western States, before the enactment of a national banking law.

[19] *Jack Brag* by Theodore Hook appeared in England in 1837, and *Rory O'More* (the novel, not the ballad, which was published in 1826) by Samuel Lover in the same year.

"While on the subject of Novels we will advert to one announced by you, 'Barnaby Rudge.' Our agent may have made some arrangement for this work with you or your publisher, should he not, he will be pleased to communicate with you on the subject for early sheets and we trust that he may make some arrangement that will be to your advantage and that will open a door for further communications."

To this Dickens replied:

"48 Doughty Street Mecklenburgh Square, London.

"October 26, 1837

" *Gentlemen:*—

"I owe you an apology for not having returned an earlier reply to your obliging letter. I was not in London when it arrived, and have been so much engaged since my return that for a short time it escaped my recollection.

"I need scarcely say that it affords me great pleasure to hear of the popularity of the Pickwick Papers in America—a country in which in common with most Englishmen, I take a high interest, and with which I hope one day to become better acquainted.

"I should not feel under the circumstances, quite at ease in drawing upon you for the amount you so liberally request me to consider you my debtors in, but I shall have very great pleasure in receiving from you an American copy of the Work, which coupled with your very handsome letter, I shall consider a sufficient acknowledgment of the American sale.

"The novel Barnaby Rudge of which you speak will not be published until late in the Autumn of next year.[20] Oliver Twist will appear in June next. I shall be very happy to enter into any arrangements with you for the transmission of early proofs of the latter book if I should hear from you that you consider it desirable.

I am, Gentlemen,
Very faithfully yours,

Mess. Carey & Co.   CHARLES DICKENS."

From this attitude of good will towards American publishers, Dickens was to depart widely in the next five years;[21] for all authors, American and British, soon saw that such conditions could not endure, and, aided by many of the publishers, they began the long and bitter fight for an international copyright

[20] It was not published until 1841.
[21] See Appendix IX.

law which was not to meet with the slightest success until 1891.

That these two great nations, Great Britain and America, had so long failed to act to their own advantage in protecting such an important class as the producers of literature, authors and publishers, was not due to any unusual stupidity nor to any exceptional meanness on the side of interested parties. The evolution of the international copyright, with all of its errors, inexcusable to us of the twentieth century, wise in our freedom from the pitfalls of the pathfinder, can be paralleled in the growth of many of the legal and social codes that hold together, more or less inadequately, the jarring interests of discordant nations.

To the bard who sang of the deeds of Beowulf,[22] to the monk as he bent over his desk in the Monastery of San Marco and copied the vision of his great fellow townsman, or, what is more probable, illuminated with loving care the acts of the church fathers, a copyright was a thing unknown and undesired. The one cared little who learned his song; the other was only anxious that the miracles of his order should be received by men as widely as possible.

But when Gutenberg invented printing in 1451, if a mooted point may be waived, a new influence had come into literature; and with the greatly increased number of copies of a literary work thereby made possible, a new commercial value for author and for publisher, was set for literary wares, and a long struggle began for legal protection for an output of human energy which had scarcely, if at all, been recognized as property before.

The first evidence of a copyright comes to us in the Renaissance in connection with the spread of the classics. Probably the first compiled and carefully edited text to be printed was an edition of Cicero's *Offices,* issued by Fust and Schöffer in 1465.[23] A rival press issued an edition at a much lower price, because upon them had not fallen the expense of preparing a

[22] Mr. Ker seems to think that no bard ever did sing of the deeds of Beowulf. (See his *The Dark Ages,* New York, 1904, pp. 250–1.)

[23] Brander Matthews, " The Evolution of the Copyright," in *The Question of Copyright,* compiled by George Haven Putnam, New York, 1891, p. 14. The article is reprinted from the *Political Science Quarterly* of November, 1890.

text. Already there were pirates in the publishing world. John of Spira was wiser four years later, in 1469, for he secured from the Venetian Republic the exclusive right for five years to print the epistles of Cicero and of Pliny.[24] The first recorded case of a copyright given directly to an author is that of Peter of Ravenna, who in 1491 secured the exclusive right to put his *Phoenix* upon the market from Venice.[25] Other Italian states followed the leadership of Venice in this matter. The earliest protection granted in Germany to a literary work was to Conrad Celtes for the work of a nun of the Benedictine cloister of Gardersheim, in 1501.[26] Luther's translation of the Bible was issued at Wittenberg in 1534 under the protection of the Elector of Saxony. By the middle of the seventeenth century, there were decrees in many of the German states by which protection could be secured. By an enactment at Berlin in 1794 protection was granted by all German states, except Wurtemburg and Mecklenburg, to both German and foreign authors whose works were represented at the book fairs of Leipzig and Frankfort.[27] True it was not very effective, as Schiller and Goethe might well testify, but it established a precedent, and seems to be the first real step towards international copyright. In France but one edition was at first protected by each copyright.

But the country in which we are most interested for the moment is Great Britain. The privilege of exclusive production was first extended in England to Richard Pynson, in 1518. The title page of Pynson's book says that no one else could print or import it for two years.[28] But Pynson was the king's printer, and similar rights were not extended to an author until twelve years later, when they were granted to John Palsgrave, on his French grammar, for seven years. In 1553 Wynkyn

---

[24] *Ibid.*, p. 15.

[25] R. R. Bowker, *Copyright, Its Law and Its Literature,* New York, 1886, p. 4.

[26] Geo. Haven Putnam, "Literary Property, An Historical Sketch," in *The Question of Copyright,* p. 47. Cf. also Bowker, p. 4.

[27] Putnam, p. 48.

[28] Matthews, p. 16.

8

de Worde obtained protection for his Witinton's *Grammar,* which had been pirated.

It will be noted that the dates given above fall within the days of the Renaissance and of the Reformation, a period of great political and religious ferment. Governments, therefore, began to exercise restrictive powers over printing, and copyright and censorship became confused. The Stationers' Company, chartered in 1556 by Philip and Mary, had for its object the prevention of the spread of the Protestant Reformation.[29] It is not necessary here to enter into the complicated relations between governmental censorship and copyright in Great Britain from this year until the period, comparatively recent, when copyright ceased to be a matter of politics. In spite of the exercise of arbitrary power, the struggle was won, or almost so, by the time that the American colonies threw off the yoke of the mother country.

The time, then, and the democratic attitude of the people, together with a thirst for knowledge and a desire for its encouragement, rendered easy an acknowledgment of literary property within the nation. The first act in the United States was passed by Connecticut in January, 1783. Massachusetts followed in March of the same year, Virginia in 1785, and New York and New Jersey in 1786.[30] These acts were primarily due to the persistency of one man, Noah Webster, and his *Speller* was the first book protected. Webster became a familiar figure at state capitols as he passed from state to state electioneering for his favorite measure. His work caused similar action to be contemplated by Rhode Island, Pennsylvania, Delaware, Maryland, and South Carolina until the necessity of state laws was done away with by the national law of May 31, 1790. But the sentiment which crystallized in this law was evoked largely by Webster's personal influence and writings.

The state legislation enacted before May, 1783, had granted a period of twenty-one years, but in May, in response to a

[29] Eaton S. Drone, *A Treatise on the Law of Property in Intellectual Productions in Great Britain and the United States,* Boston, 1879, p. 56. But compare page 21, note.

[30] *Ibid.,* p. 89.

resolution by Madison, Congress in urging copyright upon the states named fourteen years as the limit. When the general government legislated upon the matter it unfortunately chose the shorter term proposed by Madison, but if the author were living when the copyright expired it could be renewed for fourteen additional years. This was the law until 1831, when twenty-eight years were granted with the privilege of renewal for fourteen years, if the author, his widow, or his children were still living at the expiration of the first term.

There was at first an attempt to secure a perpetual copyright. It was contended that the man's literary property was as entirely his own as the faculties of his mind, and that the labor employed in its production was his exclusively. Noah Webster, in a letter to Daniel Webster, dated September 30, 1826, in arguing for perpetual, or at least a greatly extended copyright law, says: " If anything can justly give a man an exclusive right to the occupancy and enjoyment of a thing it must be the fact that he *made* it. The right of a farmer or mechanic to the exclusive enjoyment and right of disposal of what he *makes* or *produces* is never questioned. What, then, can make a difference between the produce of *muscular strength* and the produce of the intellect? "[31] Tho Webster's position seems logical, the fact remains that most of those countries which have experimented with a perpetual copyright—Holland, Belgium, Sweden, Denmark, Mexico, and some of the South American countries, have most usually speedily returned to protection for a term of years. There seems to have been an underlying feeling that a perpetual copyright would tend to build up a literary monopoly in the hands of publishers which, because of extortionate prices, would be detrimental to the spread of enlightenment in succeeding generations. What the real effect would be, whether the law of supply and demand would exercise a controlling and leveling power over it, is a question that cannot be answered, because there has never been any adequate test. Legislation has been influenced, also, by

[31] Horace E. Scudder, *Noah Webster,* Boston, 1882, p. 58. A summary of Webster's entire activity in the matter of copyright is given in pages 52 to 67.

the possibility that the heirs might possess themselves of a copyright in order to suppress a work. The fortunes of Calvin's *Institutes* in the hands of intolerant Catholic heirs might be an example.

It has just been noticed that the first steps toward international copyright were taken by the German states in 1794. There are several reasons why such should have been the case, but those which most nearly concern the present discussion are the facts of a practically similar language and a similar attitude towards life among them and a lack of international hostility, such as has until recently characterized the attitude of France and Great Britain. The first condition makes piracy easy of perpetration; it is not necessary to translate or to adapt to the spirit of an alien race. The brotherhood of man has assumed a deeper and a fuller meaning since 1794, but even now how often does the foreigner receive the full consideration of a native?

When, in 1837, the first recorded step towards international copyright was taken in the United States, both these influences were powerfully at work. British literature offered a tempting field for exploitation, and our countrymen were, in far too many cases, not in any mood to apply the golden rule to the country they had twice fought on land and sea. But in this year those conditions which have already been described forced affairs to a climax. On February 13, 1837, between fifty and sixty of the most prominent British authors presented a petition to Congress asking for protection.[32] The petition was presented to the Senate by Henry Clay. It was referred to a select committee, consisting of Clay, Preston, Buchanan, Webster, and Ewing. Their report—written, perhaps, by their chairman, Clay, for the petition was drafted by him—says, in part:

" It being established that literary property is entitled to legal protection, it results that this protection ought to be afforded wherever the property is situated. A British merchant brings

---

[32] *Executive Documents of the House of Representatives,* Second session of the 24th Congress, Washington, 1837, Vol. 4, doc. No. 162. Reprinted in the *Congressional Record,* 50th Congress, 1st Session, Washington, 1888, Vol. 19, pt. 4, p. 3241.

or transmits to the United States a bale of merchandise, and the moment it comes within the jurisdiction of our laws, they throw around it effectual security. But if the work of a British author is brought to the United States, it may be appropriated by any resident here, and republished without any compensation whatever being made to the author. We should all be shocked if the law tolerated the least invasion of the rights of property in the case of the merchandise, whilst those which justly belong to the works of authors are exposed to daily violations, without the possibility of their invoking the aid of the laws."

The committee therefore recommended that protection be granted to the authors of Great Britain and Ireland and to France, countries in which the copyrights of Americans were protected at this period. It is but equity, they said farther, that it be given to all other countries. The bill was presented in the Senate five times. Only one vote was taken, however, and that in the year 1840, which resulted in the bill being ordered to lie upon the table.

Between 1837 and 1842 numerous petitions favoring international copyright and signed by nearly all prominent British and American writers were presented to Congress. In 1838, immediately after the passing of the first international copyright act in Great Britain, Lord Palmerston invited the American government to enter into a copyright agreement between the two countries.[33] Two years later, Cornelius Matthews and George P. Putnam each issued pamphlets in favor of international copyright. The title of the latter's contribution, which appears to be the first published in the United States, is *An Argument in Behalf of International Copyright;* in its preparation he was aided by Dr. Francis Lieber. In 1843 Putnam drafted a memorial which was signed by ninety-seven publishers and printers and presented to Congress. A pamphlet in answer to this was issued at Philadelphia in the same year. Its argument was that copyright prevented the adaptation of English books to American purposes.

In 1843 too appeared one of the most eloquent of the many

[33] Geo. Haven Putman, "Literary Property, "in *The Question of the Copyright,* New York 1891, p. 96.

contributions to the discussion, one would fain believe from
the pen of William Cullen Bryant, under the title of *Address
to the People of the United States in behalf of the American
Copyright Club,* signed by Bryant, Francis L. Hawks, and Cornelius Matthews.

" The reading public of the United States," it runs, " —you,
the people of the country—have had no voice in determining
what works should be taken and what left, of all those cast
upon your shores. You have been held in pupilage, and had
your reading put upon you by the taste, or interest, or rashness,
of such as took the business of republication in charge. Even
they have not formed a permanent body, like the booksellers,
but have sprung up and died off, two or half a dozen a week,
in every city in the country. Having no settled interest in the
pursuit, grown to it and fashioned for it by no previous training, they have dealt with the vending of books in the veriest
and sorriest spirit of trading and huckstering. Eager for the
sale of the hour, calculating on no permanent connection with
one particular class of the public, they have foisted upon the
purchasers whatever the counter afforded, crying it up as the
choicest of the market, ready, the next day, to thrust it out of
sight for the newcomer of still choicer pretensions. Certain
books of a noxious character being found to hit the appetite of
certain readers, others of a broader stamp, in a like view, have
been produced from foreign tongues, and distributed by the
thousand and ten thousand. The foreign supply coming short,
native writers, of an easy conscience, have been put in training,
to try themselves upon whatever is coarsest and vilest. In the
general hurly-burly works of this texture have escaped from
the by-ways and alleys where they were first hatched, and flare,
in broad-day, in the placards and windows of bookdealers,
whose sense of propriety could have only faltered in a general
decay of right opinion among the people at large."[34]

The pamphlet complains bitterly of the attitude of the press,
which venally writes and publishes misleading criticisms of the
ephemeral publications of the times. This, they point out, is
really suicide, for the taste of the people is in danger of being
so vitiated and so fixed in the channel of the cheap serial

[34] *Address to the People of the United States in behalf of the American
Copyright Club Adopted at New York, October 18, 1843.* New York, 1843.
This is an octavo pamphlet of eighteen pages signed by William Cullen
Bryant, Francis L. Hawks, and Cornelius Matthews, pp. 9–10.

adapted publication that the press would eventually languish for lack of patronage. The American author, they write, is in danger of disappearing, and with him many wholesome aspects of our nationality. The ballad singers and men of literature in the days of old nerved their countrymen up to deeds of moral and physical heroism, but no amount of cheap foreign literature will ever inspirit the Americans as Americans to fight the battles of their country in court and mart, on field and flood. Whether or not Bryant wrote the Address, it is worthy of notice in passing that until his death he did yeoman service in the cause of international copyright, thru the columns of the *Evening Post;* and he thus fixed the policy of this paper, which contended for the cause until the victory was gained. But he continued his efforts in other ways, for in 1848, in company with John Gay, George P. Putnam and others he returned to the attack, presenting in this year a petition which never got further than the select committee to which it was referred. In 1853, to continue this chronicle as briefly as possible, Charles Sumner, then Chairman of the Senate Committee on Foreign Affairs, reported to the Senate a treaty which Everett, then Secretary of State, had drawn up. It was reported favorably by the Committee on Foreign Affairs. While this treaty was before Congress, five publishing houses of New York addressed a letter to Everett suggesting an agreement practically identical with the one now in force.[35] In 1858 an International Copyright Bill was introduced by Edward Jay Morris of Pennsylvania, but no notice was taken of it.

Bryant once more entered the arena in 1868, when there was issued a circular letter, *Justice to Authors and Artists,* calling for a meeting to organize an international copyright association. A meeting was held on April 9, at which he presided. The Copyright Association for the Protection and Advancement of Literature and Art was organized, with Bryant as president, and E. C. Stedman as secretary. The object of the Association was "to promote the enactment of a just and suitable international copyright law for the benefit of authors

[35] Geo. Haven Putnam, "Literary Property" in *The Question of Copyright,* New York, 1891, p. 67.

and artists in all parts of the world." One hundred and fifty-three signatures were secured, one hundred and one were authors, and nineteen were publishers.[36]

In 1872 the new Library Committee asked all those interested in the matter to assist in framing a bill. A meeting of publishers was held in New York. But even yet, in spite of thirty-seven years of agitation, the friends of international copyright seemed hopelessly disorganized, for four reports and two individual suggestions were submitted to the Committee. The Harper Company, moreover, presented, thru their counsel, a letter, which, among other arguments against the bill, said that "any measure of international copyright was objectionable because it would add to the price of books, and thus interfere with the education of the people.[37] Senator Lot M. Morrill, chairman, reported adversely because of the lack of unanimity of opinion among those interested. Perhaps a brief quotation from his report will be of interest as showing the attitude of a large number of our congressmen at this period. He maintained that "an international copyright was not called for by reasons of general equity or of constitutional law; that the adoption of any plan which had been proposed would be of very doubtful advantage to American authors, and would not only be an unquestionable and permanent injury to the interests engaged in the manufacture of books, but a hindrance to the diffusion of knowledge among the people and to the cause of American education."[38]

The lack of coördination among the friends of international copyright was largely removed in 1883 when the American Copyright League was organized and began an active campaign to arouse popular sentiment. Perhaps they were largely responsible for the fact that in 1884 and in 1885 the annual messages of President Arthur and of President Cleveland contained strong recommendations for the passage of some sort of international copyright bill.

[36] *Ibid.*, p. 68.
[37] *Ibid.*, p. 70.
[38] *Congressional Record*, 50th Congress, 1st session, Vol. 19, pt. 4, Washington, 1888, p. 3511.

On January 21, 1886, the twelfth international copyright bill was introduced into the Senate by Chase of Rhode Island. The Senate Committee on Patents took careful testimony from friends and foes in four public hearings.[39] The Chase bill marked an important turning point in the history of the struggle. The long educational campaign was producing fruit. It was no longer a question whether or not there should be international copyright, but merely what form it should take.

But the friends of the measure did not rest. The American Publishers' Copyright League was organized in 1887. The Executive Committee of this league was given instructions to coöperate with the American Copyright League, which was composed of authors. A Conference Committee was immediately formed of the executive committees of the two leagues, and this body took the leadership in all the work done between 1887 and 1891. Copyright leagues were formed in Boston, Chicago, St. Louis, Cincinnati, Minneapolis, Denver, Buffalo, Colorado Springs, and in many other places. Missionary work was carried on with such zeal that the public conscience began to be aroused. The matter was taken up in the pulpit; *The National Sin of Piracy,* a classic of its kind, by the Rev. Henry Van Dyke of New York, was widely circulated. The press, secular and religious, made international copyright a question of the day.

Authors gave what were called "author's readings," in which the leading American writers read selections from their

[39] Mr. Dana Estes, of the Boston firm of Estes, Lauriat & Co., said at one of these hearings: "For two years past tho I belong to a publishing house that emits nearly $1,000,000 worth of books per year, I have absolutely refused to entertain the idea of publishing an American manuscript. I have returned many scores, if not hundreds, of manuscripts of American authors, unopened even, simply from the fact that it is impossible to make the books of most American authors pay, unless they are first published and acquire recognition through the columns of the magazines. Were it not for that one saving opportunity of the great American magazines which are now the leading ones of the world and have an international reputation and circulation, American authorship would be at a still lower ebb than at present." (*Senate Reports,* 1st Session, 49th Congress, 1885–86, Washington, 1886, Vol. 7, Report No. 1188, p. 53.) Mr. Henry Holt made a very similar speech at the same time.

own works. These were widely attended and served as effect-ive advertisements of their cause, while the receipts aided in the expense of the campaign. Among those who took part in these readings were Eggleston, Stedman, Stoddard, Gilder, Stockton, Bunner, Cable, Page, Julian Hawthorne, and Harris.

Such is the outline of the struggle for protection by Amer-ican and British authors, aided finally by practically every im-portant American publisher, for even the Harpers had radically changed their views since 1872. What then were those potent forces working against international copyright which so long defeated every attempt?

One of the strongest influences has already been indicated— ignorance and apathy on the subject. The large majority of the Americans were indifferent. They did not at first see clearly the moral obliquity inherent in the purchase of a pirated volume, or the serious injury they were doing to American nationality when they failed to encourage the American author by buying his book. They did not see the danger of the loss of national ideals thru the reading of cheap books entirely at variance with the democratic and social fiber of our lives, which formed an alarming proportion of the reading of the masses. On these points our national conscience was not dead but only sleeping to awaken at the earnest call of those of clearer vision, who were to show the people that, as Lowell put it, "There is one thing better than a cheap book, and that is a book honestly come by"; and, he might have added, one that bears an honest message.

The measure was regarded by some as class legislation and as monopolistic in character. The question of copyright was very early confused with that of the protective tariff. The protectionists were those most opposed to the measure. At first sight it looks as though the exact opposite should have been the case, for the American author was but asking that the product of his labor should be protected from imported goods upon which no duty (copyright) had been paid, but which had been simply "appropriated"; and that he be not undersold. What troubled the protectionists, however, was the possibility that if the privilege of selling books were granted to foreigners, they might be printed abroad; and thus the mechanical features of the production of books assumed a much more important aspect in their eyes than the intellectual and spiritual side. The binding was worth more than the content, the ink than the idea. Indeed the final treaty was for a while in danger because of the opposition of the Typographical Union. The same attitude had been present in Great Britain. Mr. William H. Appleton, in defense of himself and the American people, made the charge that Great Britain had never offered the United States a treaty shaped merely for the protection of the author, but that "it is really an authors' and publishers' copyright that is demanded of us—Every arrangement that England has hitherto offered is but a kind of legal saddle for the English publisher to ride his author into the American book-market."[40]

Philadelphia was the chief center of opposition to an international copyright agreement, tho to a Philadelphian, Henry C. Lea, was due the wording of the typesetting and non-importation clauses, the insertion of which bridged the gap between authors and publishers and made the final treaty possible. Mr. Henry Carey Baird of Philadelphia was the leader of the opposition, and the most able exponent of the advantages of existing conditions. In 1872 he presided over a meeting held at Philadelphia at which the following resolutions were adopted:

"1. That thought, unless expressed, is the property of the thinker; when given to the world, it is, as light, free to all. 2. As property it can only demand the protection of the municipal laws of the country to which the thinker is subject. 3. The author of any country, by becoming a citizen of this, and assuming and performing the duties thereof, can have the same protection than an American author has. 4. The trading of privileges to foreign authors for privileges to be granted to Americans is not just, because the interest of others than themselves may be sacrificed thereby. 5. Because the good of the whole people, and the safety of republican institutions, demand that books shall not be made costly for the

[40] William H. Appleton, *Letters on International Copyright,* New York, 1872. Pamphlet, octavo, pp. 25, p. 7.

multitude by giving the power to foreign authors to fix their price here as well as abroad."[41]

This quotation shows concisely the views held by the opponents of international copyright law, tho Mr. Baird omits one important argument, put forth by his allies, that such a law would hinder adaptation. No evidence is obtainable that the first half of the first proposition met with a very indignant denial. The second half embodies a confusion of form and content which was especially prevalent during the entire discussion. Probably the facts of Von Holst's history are common property, as Mr. Baird argues, but the person who makes too liberal use of his facts plus his form is apt to repent.

It is not necessary to discuss each of these articles, but the last one is of especial importance; for what popular opposition there was to international copyright is largely embodied in it. Books whose influence were for the "good of the whole people" were, it is safe to say now, not really made more costly. "Libraries" or series of books, composed overwhelmingly of fiction taken without compensation from the works of British authors, did furnish cheap reading. New numbers of these pirated series appeared sometimes as often as twice a week. It can be readily imagined what class of fiction was necessarily published when it was issued at that rate. Anything would do to fill in. Other classes of books, those that needed careful and accurate printing and illustration were seldom printed, for the reputable publisher knew that a cheaper pirated edition, no matter what its imperfections, might cause an actual loss on his conscientious production.

"Adaptation," mentioned above, was one of the war cries of the opposition. An international copyright law, they argued, would prevent British books on such subjects as theology, education, and law from being modified to meet American conditions.

"Adaptation" particularly excited the ire of the British

[41] Geo. Haven Putnam, "Literary Property," in *The Question of the Copyright,* New York, 1891, p. 73. The passage may not be a direct quotation, as it is not so indicated. I have been unable to identify it.

writers, tho the danger of mutilation was far greater in the case of the Americans. Much more often did a dash of the proof-reader's pen across the title page rob the latter of that glory to which Lord Camden himself thought they were entitled. Even at a very early period British writers were too well known and too widely read for garbled versions to go undetected, and once detected, the public demanded a correct copy. That exquisite literary gem, the footnote in which Mistress Anne Hunter so sweetly explains just why she came to write Freneau's *Death Song of a Cherokee Indian*,[42] could hardly have been produced, and afterwards stumbled over by two editors, in America, where a more intimate acquaintance with British literature would have caused the immediate discovery of a corresponding theft.

To name but one example: in 1796 one Mr. Prigmore attempted to produce *The School for Citizens* which he had altered without acknowledgment from a British comedy.[43] The mistake in judgment was atrocious: had he merely adapted Kotzebue, as did Dunlap himself, he would have received approbation instead of excoriation. The struggle of the American playwright against the exploitation of foreign authors was even more bitter and desperate than had been that of the novelist; for in their case they must take the field against English, French, and German. Mr. Wilkins has found fifty-six works of Kotzebue alone reprinted in this country between 1799 and 1826. Scribe and other French dramatists soon reached America, and what these two countries could not supply could be secured in England. The financial reasons of the publishers for preferring British novels were multiplied four fold for the stage manager in the case of a tested play. In 1814 a dealer at Baltimore writes that his sales of British plays amount to $400 per year. Nothing is said about the sales of American playwrights. Miller, January 10, 1821, offers Barry Cornwall's *Mirandola* to Carey, but adds that he

[42] Moses Coit Tyler, *The Literary History of the American Revolution*, New York, 1897, Vol. I, p. 179.

[43] William Dunlap, *A History of the American Theater*, New York, 1832, p. 197.

is engaged to furnish Mr. Price of New York and Warren & Wood of Philadelphia with early copies for the use of their respective theaters. Munden and Thompson of New York approach Carey, in April, 1821, for an exchange of plays. They have, they write, arranged to receive from London new plays which they wish to offer to the theaters of both cities.

The general attitude of theatrical managers is summed up in a letter by William B. Wood of Baltimore, who writes, May 17, 1821: "As to Lord Byron's Tragedy,[44] we are all impatience to see it, altho it was announced as a non actable drama. However, if it is *possible* to make it a night's entertainment it shall go hard but we shall do it." A great name as well as a great success was evidently enough to impress an American stage manager. The stream of transatlantic plays that flowed into America was as continuous as that of the novels, tho from more varied sources. Whether or not it accounts for the non-appearance of a great dramatic genius is a matter of mere conjecture: that it lessened the productions of talent is a fact.

It should be added that, ending with 1850, the British laws had been interpreted so as to protect the American author. The simple sense of justice, however, did not come strongly enough to Americans as a nation to enable them to meet this attitude half way and to settle the matter thus early. And so to the incalculable detriment of both British and Americans the matter was allowed to take the destructive course which has just been sketched.

But the optimist who is looking for comfort in this dreary warfare, other than that the struggle was finally won, can find it in the progress of the magazine. Two letters have been quoted, one to Poe and one to Simms, which explain better than pages of theorizing its advantages and its dangers. The "mammoth Weeklies" we see had aided greatly in decreasing the popularity of Simms.[45] In the case of a writer who had

[44] Byron published four in this year.
[45] Simms' first volume of prose (*Martin Faber,* 1833) was a collection of short stories. Then follow twelve novels (not counting *The Book of My Lady,* 1833, a collection of stories) which appear up to 1842. In 1844

no talent for the short story there was no compensation; but when Poe writes a comparatively unpopular *Narrative of Arthur Pym*,[46] and later finds no publisher for his " new collection of Tales," he can return to improving the short story and (as a corollary) to building up the magazines. Just what influence such conditions exerted in turning the genius of Poe away from the novel and keeping it in the channel of the short story probably no one is qualified to state. When, however, we consider the writer of talent we have something more than hypothesis. Mr. Estes, in the speech quoted from on page 105, cited Miss Murfree (" Charles Egbert Craddock ") as an example of an exquisite talent that would never have been known had it not been for the saving influence of the magazine. And for obvious reasons are we not inclined to underestimate in our survey of literature the potency of the men and women just under genius?

Such a saving influence to talent and to latent genius it was that Mathew Carey exerted in America from 1784 to 1839. In those hundreds of thousands of letters and accounts that represent his publishing activity from 1787 to 1823, and in the glimpse we get of his successors, sons and grandsons, in the letters between 1834 and 1837 and between 1841 and 1842, are contained hints of hopes and anxieties that animated a long line of his contemporaries, business men as well as literary. Here are names long ago in oblivion's dust, names that are fast going thither, and names that will live forever. Franklin, Washington, Lafayette, and Jefferson had occasion to address him. Dwight, Freneau, Belknap, Mrs. Rowson, Noah Webster, Irving, Miss Davidson, Neal, Cooper, Poe, Simms, and Dickens sought him as a publisher, in many cases as a personal friend. Weems relieves his querulousness in many a

appears *The Prima Donna*, a short story, and after this period the extraordinary array of two-volume novels is broken in a remarkable manner. In 1836 he begins his chief contributions, of a critical nature largely, to the magazines. (William P. Trent, *William Gilmore Simms*, Boston, 1892, pp. 335–341.) It appears that Simms is trying to adapt himself to the literary conditions of the country.

[46] It seems to have had a better reception in England, where it was republished in 1838, 1841, and 1861.

painful quire, Dabney[47] defends his translation of *Eugene* against the critics with a fervor that softens the adjacent seals; while letter after letter that has little or no relation to business shows how widely Carey's name had penetrated and how much trust was reposed in his judgment and tenderness of heart. When Thomas and Andrews, his first great rivals, hesitate or refuse to publish the works of an unknown author, he ventures, on account of the patriotism in his warm Irish nature, in behalf of the struggling or the obscure writer. Genius can generally care for itself, but the talent of the country greatly needed such a friend as it found in Mathew Carey. Exactly how much he influenced the production of American literature can be told only by that deeply psychological study which determines just how far the writers that will live in our literature used the minor ones, which he alone encouraged, to build upon, and to what extent they themselves would otherwise have succumbed to untoward circumstances. But surely his influence must have been far more potent than that of many a writer whose biography has long adorned our libraries. We have firm ground under our feet as we turn from the producer to the consumer. When the history of literary culture in America is written no small praise must be given to the man who caused books and all their attendant blessings to penetrate even beyond the Mississippi while yet the Indian disputed possession with the white man.

[47] Richard Dabney (1787–1825) was born in Louisa County, Virginia. His early schooling was neglected, but at the age of about sixteen he began to study the classics and made rapid progress. In 1811 he was injured by the burning of the Richmond theater, opium was prescribed and he became a slave to the habit and also to strong drink. His *Poems, Original and Translated* were published in a thin duodecimo volume at Richmond in 1812. It was not popular, and the author attempted to suppress it. In 1815 an enlarged edition containing translations from the Greek and the Latin and showing considerable scholarship and power of expression was published, by Carey, at Philadelphia. For this volume Carey paid him $40. He was employed quite frequently by Carey as a translator, proofreader and collector of literary materials. In the latter capacity he gave considerable aid in the production of the *Olive Branch*. A long series of letters from him is found in the correspondence for 1814.

There has been no sustained attempt in this study to bring out the inspiring patriotism of the man; and no fully adequate one to show his lovable nature; for his name ranks high among American philanthropists. Perhaps Poe, who knew him personally, has given the best estimate of his character in his review of Carey's *Autobiography*[48] when he says that " In the whole private and public course of Mr. Mathew Carey the strictest scrutiny can detect nothing derogatory to the character of ' the noblest work of God, an honest man.' "[49]

[48] Published in *The New England Magazine,* Boston, 1833–4, Vols. 5, 6, 7.

[49] *The Southern Literary Messenger,* Richmond, 1836, Vol. II, p. 203.

APPENDIX I

William Cobbett, after his return to England, in June, 1800, set up, under encouragement from the government, his *Weekly Register* which afterwards became famous. But he changed rapidly from Toryism to Radicalism. Among the memories of America that he took back with him was that of the liberty of the press. When he threw himself with such ardor into the reform movements which culminated later in the Reform Bill of 1832 and in the Corn Laws he sought aid in America in direct contributions from the pens of other writers as well as in the republication of his own articles. Then it was that he recalled his former enemy, who, on his side, was always willing to forgive and to fight under the banner of any man who sought to better the conditions of the human race. Carey won him other friends in this country, notable among whom was Richard Rush.

Later, in 1817, when Cobbett's long fight for political and social betterment had aroused the wrath of a reactionary and unscrupulous ministry, he was forced to flee to America, where he remained until November, 1819.[1] Just before leaving he wrote " Mr. Cobbett's Taking Leave of his Countrymen," which appeared in the *Weekly Register* for April 5, 1817.

" If I remain here," he says, " I must *cease to write,* either from compulsion, or from a sense of duty to my countrymen; therefore it is impossible to do any good to the cause of my country by remaining in it; but, if I remove to a country where I can write with perfect freedom, it is not only *possible,* but very *probable,* that I shall, sooner or later, be able to render that cause important and lasting service . . . *I can serve that cause no longer by remaining here;* but the cause itself is so good, so just, so manifestly right and virtuous, and has been combated by means so unusual, so unnatural and so violent, that it *must triumph in the end."*

[1] See p. 118.

(W. Cobbett to M. Carey)
BOTLEY, NEAR SOUTHAMPTON, 16 July, 1815.
Dear Sir,

I thank you for the little work, which you have been so good as to send me, and of which, you may be assured, I shall make the best use in my power. We have now lived to see the necessity of a secure and hearty co-operation between the friends of wisdom in *all* countries, and especially those of England and America. Terrible as things seem here; bent, as we appear to be, upon rooting out the very fibers of freedom all over the earth, there are many, very many, good men in England; excellent minds; and what now appears outwardly to be the sweeping *triumph* of tyranny, is, in fact, a desperate *struggle* of tyranny, whose monstrous exertions must finally defeat herself, and in dealing blows against whom *you* have been very successful. Your two works contain much information, peculiarly useful to me.. The Olive Branch has found its way to me from Boston. Situated, as I am, at such a distance from London, I have few opportunities of sending anything to America; but if you will point out anything that I can do for you, I will, if within my power, do it. I now do myself the pleasure to send you a Copy of Mr. Birkbeck's Tour in France last year; very well worth your reading.

I perceive, that there are some writers in America, and one or two amongst the friends of freedom, who delight in reminding their readers, that I once labored to an end, the opposite of that, at which I now aim. That the seekers after titles and tyranny should act thus, is, by no means, surprising; but, there are two good causes, which ought to restrain the latter: *justice to me, and good to the world.* As to the former, ought it not to be bourne in mind, that youth, inexperience, prejudice of education, concurring with the universal abuse of my native country, at the time, were quite sufficient to account for an ardent mind taking a wrong bias and obstinately persevering therein, especially under that *legal persecution* which I am always ready to assert, that I endured in America. If I have been brought round by the feeling of greater persecution and by that alone; admit this to be the fact, what is there *faulty* in it? For what do men live, but to grow wiser?

For what is experience but to correct their errors? Then, as to the latter cause; ought not the friends of freedom in America to reflect, that, though they may, in some small degree, lessen the effect of my writings by their conduct above mentioned, they can thereby only do so much harm to the cause, which those writings are so well calculated to aid. For my part, I have recollections of the past errors or past hostility of those who *now* tug at the same oar with myself. With a great facility at writing; with a stock of experience such as few men possess; with a mass of information collected from all sources; with great disposition to labour; and with health such as falls to the lot of not one man out of ten thousand, to which add easy circumstances and an obedient family of promising children; few men have such power to do good in the cause of mankind. This good I am endeavoring to do. This must be clear to every man in America. It is, therefore, to say the least of it, very silly and waspish to carp at the errors of 1796. As to the ruffians who *still* affect to think that I was once in the *way of this government* they are beneath notice. However, after all, these carpings will have no effect worth speaking of. Twenty years experience has taught me, that people will read that which is written to their taste, and that, sooner or later, reason and truth will prevail, if they are put before sensible people in a way to be clearly understood.

I congratulate you most heartily upon the defeat of the Royal Pirates of the Straights by your gallant Navy.[2] Even *this* is a blow against general tyranny. Even *this* inculcates the excellence of your political institutions, and tends to extend the effects of your example. Be *united;* concede a little on both sides amongst yourselves; and you will be not only happy and free but, will make other nations the same.

To Mr. M. Carey
    Philadelphia.

I am, dear sir,
      Your most obedt sert
        WM. COBBETT.

(W. Cobbett to M. Carey)

LONDON, 5 January, 1816.

Dear Sir,

I am very sorry to learn, that you have not received the copy of Major Cartwright's little book. I saw him yesterday, in a few hours after I had received yours of the 17th of November, and though he has but one copy left, he has promised me, that I shall have it to send to you, to do which, *securely* I shall have an opportunity in a few weeks.

[2] *The Pride of Brittania Humbled; or, The Queen of the Ocean Un-queen'd by the American Cock-boats, etc, etc.. Illustrated and demonstrated by four Letters to Lord Liverpool* (Philadelphia, 1815) is one of the several pamphlets by Cobbett which the Americans saw fit to publish at this period.

The " Olive Branch " would have bourne, not a " small," but a " large edition "; but, it would have clapp'd the publisher, for 2 years, in Newgate, or, in some more deadly jail. *I* was afraid to cause the *Exposition* to be published; or, even *lend* it. By exciting a great deal of curiosity about it, and by throwing it in the way of a man who thought less of danger than of profit, *five editions* of it was got out. Shame appears to have restrained the arm of power upon this occasion. If one dared even to *discuss,* in the mildest way, any ticklish subject, do you think that the brave people of Ireland, could be *shut up in their houses from sunset to sunrise upon pain of transportation.*

I am very happy that you think that I have done some service to America, and still more to hear your animating description of her prosperity. If that continue, and if her sons be wise, the Despots have, even now, done nothing as to the final accomplishment of their views. The fate of freedom is yet unknown to them; and they seem to perceive it, and to give signs of their fears, every time that America is mentioned.

You, who saw England so long ago, can form no idea of the *sort of government* that we have now. The parliament of your time was a thing no more resembling that of this day, than a Greyhound resembles a Hyena. No man of any sense ever feels any interest in its proceedings. The affairs of the country are, however, drawing very fast towards a crisis. The war has left a load behind it far more dangerous to the government than any event of mere war could ever have been. Pecuniary distress has spread consternation amongst the ranks. Every one has his *remedy,* and all fear some great and terrible convulsion.

I should only put you to expense by enclosing any of my Registers; but, if some parts of the late Numbers, which I have sent out in the hope of their being republished, meet your eye, you will see that I am resolved no longer to suffer my communications with America to be interrupted by the means hitherto practiced; and from the same source, you will also learn the real situation in this country, which is *precisely,* and to the very letter, the opposite of that of America, agreeably to your description.

In a few weeks, I shall write to you again, and, I shall then send Major Cartwright's book,[3] with, perhaps, some other

[3] This was probably Major John Cartwright's *Six Letters to the Marquis of Tavistock, on a Reform of the Commons House of Parliament,* 1812. Major John Cartwright (1740–1824) entered the navy at the age of eighteen. About 1775 he began to take an active interest in political affairs,

thing or two if I meet with them worth your notice, and likely to be of use.

In the meanwhile I remain your
Most obedient and most hu— serv't.
WM. COBBETT.

(From Wm. Cobbett, Jr.)
To Mr. M. Carey,
Philadelphia.

No. 86, MAIDEN LANE, NEW YORK, 7 May. 1817

Dear Sir,

My father and brother John Morgan and myself are just arrived here, having stuck to our own country to the last hour. The former is gone to look about him a little in Long Island, but desired me to write a line by Messieurs Archambault and Rousseau, the bearers, with his kindest regards to you.—These two gentlemen were lately of Bonaparte's suite; they are two out of four that our government would not allow to remain with him at St. Helena; they came in the same ship with us from Liverpool, and are now in quest of Joseph Bonaparte. They made us very agreeable companions on board the ship, and my father wishes to be of any service he can to them as they are perfect strangers in this country, and cannot even speak the language enough to pay their way; Therefore my father would esteem it very kind of you to put them in the way of finding King Joseph's house in Philadelphia, after which they will be at home.

Hoping that yourself and Mrs. Morgan are well,
I beg you to believe me, Dear Sir,
Mr. J. Morgan   Yours very sincerely,
WM COBBETT, JR.

and became a champion of the Americans. *A Letter to Edmund Burke, controverting the Principles of American Government laid down in his lately published speech on American Taxation* is a brief in their behalf. He refused to join Lord Howe's command against America. Among the reforms he advocated were those of an annual parliament and universal suffrage; he was also an anti-slavery leader, and was called the Father of Reform. From 1803 to 1804 he contributed papers to Cobbett's *Register* on the defenseless condition of England. In 1810, 1812, and 1823 he published works on constitutional reforms. He was active in the cause of the Greeks. In. 1813 he was arrested in the course of a political tour, but released soon after. In 1820 he was tried and fined for sedition.

APPENDIX II

Stansbury, the writer of this letter, was a printer of considerable repute in his day. His date for the first use of lithography in America is worth noticing.

"NEW YORK Novem. 12. 1821

"*Dear Sir,*

"I take the liberty of sending you herewith several specimens of engraving executed in the French method on stone. With the general history of this art, now so much in use on the Continent, you are no doubt acquainted: the present I believe is the first instance of its application to any useful purpose in this Country. . . ."

ARTHUR JO. STANSBURY.

APPENDIX III

The following list is given, as indicated at page 31, as a typical order of the period about 1800. It shows that the reading of the general public at that time was of quite as ephemeral a nature as it is at present.

1 Mansion House—1 Ethelinde
1 The Abbess—1 Ivy Castle
1 Abbey of St Asaph
1 Neighborhood
1 Suzette's Dowry
4 Simple Story—4 Nature & Art
4 Melissa & Narcia
1 Banished Man—1 Desmond
2 Fool of Quality
2 Julia de Roubingre
2 Man of Feeling
2 Man of the World
2 Man as he is
2 Rasselas & Dinarbas
2 Sorrows of Edith
2 Arabian Tales *Complete*
1 Eliosa
2 Count de Saulene
2 Sophia Sternheim
2 Fille de Chambre
1 Lucinda Courtney
2 Natural Daughter
2 Vicar of Wakefield
2 Madame Ricobina's Letters
? Nettley Abbey
2 Haunted Priory
2 Welch Neices
2 Agnes de Courci
1 Ned Evans
1 The Farmer of Englewood
2 House of Junian
1 Hugh Nevor

APPENDIX IV

The following bill not only indicates, as suggested on page fifty-three what German books were making their way to America as early as 1816, but also the cost of the current literature, and the difficulty of collecting a small order in Germany. In this case some of the books had to be ordered from Weimar and from Leipsic.

BOUGHT FOR MATTH CAREY BY PROFESSOR EBELING
Hamburgh May 1816.

	Current	Marks	Shill.
6 German Bibles in Folio with Plates. Price at Lunenburg		96	14
Freight from Lunenburg		1	12
Perthes's total	ms	98	19
Agnes von Lilien		7	8
Babo neue Schauspiele		3	
Bertucks Bilderbuch fur Kinder Nr. 1 to 158 at 1 M each		156	
Text explaining it. Nr. 1 to 156		83	
Nr. 151 to 156 single		3	5
Nr. 51 of the Text wanting is already ordered from Weimar and expected every day.			
Burde Erzählungen		2	8
Hagemeister don Juan		2	
Heinse Laidion		3	
Herder's Lieder der Liebe		1	12
Hufelands Matrobiobik 2 vols.		5	8
Jing's Heinr. Stilling 5 vols.		17	8
Klinger's Faust's Leben		5	
Lafontaine Fedor u. Marie		4	8
.... Märchen, Erzählungen 2 vols		8	
.... Leben eines armer Landprediger 2 vol.		10	8
Meiners's Geschichte der Ursprung der Wissenschaften 2 vols		12	
.... Historische Vergleichung der Sitten 2 vols.		11	8
(The 3rd volume is expected daily from the Leipsic fair.) Hª.			
current ms		336	13
Milbillers Elizabeth		6	
" Komradin		4	
Kotzebues Almanach dramatischer Spiele the newest 2 volumes each		10	
Kotzebues nissischer Kreigsgefangener		3	
Crt. mks.		359	13
10 p. cent		36	13
		323	
6 Bibles		98	10
Hambr. Current mks		421	10

APPENDIX V

The following letters, except the first, which is interesting in other ways, throw some light upon the intellectual activities of Thomas Jefferson after his retirement from the presidency.

(To Mathew Carey)   WASHINGTON Jan 12th 1801
Sir
    I received some time ago your favor by Doctor Carey together with the American Monitor, for which be pleased to accept my thanks—I have no doubt of its utility as a school Book, as soon as the pupil is so far advanced as to reflect on what he reads, & that I believe is in an earlier stage than is generally imagined. I concur with you in the importance of inculcating into the minds of young people the great moral & political truths & that it is better to put into their hands Books which while they teach them to Read teach them to think also & to think soundly.
I am with great esteem
Your most obdt serv
TH JEFFERSON

Messrs Careys
Philadelphia.
(Recd July 2 Ans July 5)

MONTICELLO June 28 (18)18

Dear Sir
    Soon after the date of my letter of the 21st I received Bridgman's Index safely, and had taken for granted McMahon was coming with it, but as it did not come, I presume it has either been forgotten or is lodged by the way. in either case I ask your information & attention to it; and further that you will be so kind as to inform me whether a copy of Baron Grimm's memoirs (16 vols 8vo) can be had, and at what price? I salute you with friendship and respect
TH. JEFFERSON

Mr. M. Carey.
    The "letter of the 21st" was not found.

MONTICELLO Oct. 6. (18)18.

Dear Sir
    Your letter of Sep. 21 reached me on the 28, and the book which is the subject of it had come to hand by the preceding

122

mail. both found me recovering from a long indisposition, and not yet able to sit up to write, but in pain. The reading a 4to volume of close print is an undertaking which my ordinary occupations and habits of life would not permit me to encounter; nor under any circumstances could I arrogate to myself the office of directing or anticipating the public judgment as to the publications worthy of their attention. letters of mine, unwarily written, have been sometimes used by editors with that view, but not with my consent, but in one or two particular cases. if the vol. of Haines's you sent me be your only copy, I will return it to you. if you have another, I would willingly keep it, and be glad to receive the 2nd when it comes out. I shall be glad if you can send me by mail the 2 books undermentioned, and would rather receive them *unbound*. I see them advertised by Wells & Lilly of Boston. I salute you with sincere esteem and respect.

Griesbach: Greek testament. the 8vo and full edition.

The New Testament in an improved version on the basis of Newcome's translation.

free Th Jefferson   Free
                                    MR. MATTHEW CAREY
                                         Philadelphia

Dear Sir   MONTICELLO Nov. 28, (18)18.
                                      Recd. Dec. 4)
                                      Ans. Dec. 7
In a letter of Oct. 6 I requested the favor of you to send me Griesbach's Greek testament, the 8vo & full edition, and The New testament in an improved version on the basis of Newcome's translation which, altho published in Boston, I supposed could be had in Philadelphia.—hearing nothing of them I conjecture they are either forgotten or not to be had in Philadelphia. I would rather have them *unbound,* and they may come by mail if to be had. I salute you with friendship & respect.
                                    TH. JEFFERSON
   Mr. Carey

(To Mathew Carey)
Dear Sir   MONTICELLO July 31, (18)20
   Your favor of July 13. was received on the 21st inst. and I now enclose you 25.D. in bills of the bank of Virginia as none of the U.S. are to be had here. the surplus of 1.75 may cover the discount perhaps.
   I presume you import from time to time books from England, and should be glad if on the first occasion you would write for a copy of Baxter's history of England for me. and if there

be an 8vo edn of it, I should greatly prefer it. If none, I must be contented with the original 4to. I doubt whether it went to a 2nd edition, even the Whigs of England not bearing to see their bible, Hume, republicanized. octavo volumes suit my hand, and my shelves so much better than any other size, that if the Conversations in chemistry, mentioned below can be had from England in 8vo I would rather wait for their importation, if not I would prefer the English edition 12 mo that of Humphrey's. If J. Sinclair's book is not to be had with you it might be added to the importation. I salute you with great friendship & respect.

TH. JEFFERSON

Baxter's History of England.
Conversations in Chemistry.
Sr. John Sinclairs Code of agriculture. this is the work which is in a single vol. thick 8vo and must be distinguished from a similar work in several volumes published some years ago and of which there is a condensed digest.

Mess. M. Carey & son   MONTICELLO Aug. 14, (18)20.
(Recd Aug. 20)

I received yesterday your favor of the 5th, and by the preceding mail the Conversations in Chemistry had come to hand. I am quite content with the edition, as I shall be with the American edition of Sr. J. Sinclair's Code of agriculture. I had not before known that it had been reprinted in America. I wish that there may have been an 8vo edition of Baxter's history of England published there. if not I must be content with the 4to. order it to be well bound if you please, as I am attached to good bindings. I salute you with esteem & respect.

TH. JEFFERSON.

APPENDIX VI

BALTIMORE 26, Feb. 1822.

MESSRS. H. C. CAREY & I. LEA

Gentlemen,

I intimated to you some time ago that, when Logan, with which I had been in travail for an unprecedented time, considering my earlier habits of gestation, was fairly launched, I had a plan in view which I thought might be made profitable and honourable, to you, and myself—that plan is now mentioned. I have nearly completed a series of novels—in secrecy and darkness, while most of the good people of this world, particularly the *watchmen,* were asleep—. The *first* you have—the second and third are finished and the fourth, will be, within a month— I believe. This has been no common effort—I have bent all my power and faculties to the labour—(one line rendered illegible by the fold in the letter) . . . of my own reputation because I do not mean to be known in them—but willing while I *could,* to contribute, —, do not call me vain I have thought on what I say, and I do not lightly say it—to the reputation of my country.

The whole are materially *American*—the *second* entirely new in the design and execution—containing notices & speeches of our eminent men—actually living—native scenery, habits, etc., the *third* a tale, in which I have striven hard to counteract some prejudices natural to the mind repety deformed and dwarfish gentry manners life—etc—and the fourth, which is the last that I have written, or *shall write,* I verily believe, for neither health, duty nor profession will permit me to continue the labour, is a tale utterly woven abt the events of our Revolution artfully narrated—and with all the passion of my nature—

In the first place I can assure you that no mortal living knows of the matter thus far—: and I am determined that no one shall, if I can help it, whose interest is not as well as mine, to keep the secret. I do not mean to acknowledge them but I know well that I shall be suspected, for I have been assailed, recently, from several quarters, and even from our bench, with entreaty and persuasion to write a *novel* a poem—. —

Much of the value of the books will, of course, depend upon this secrecy, after the public are excited. Logan, I do not expect will startle them much,—(Waverly did not) but it will put them into a state of preparation—against the second shock, which I promise you, shall charge them, brim full of electricity!—the third will reduce their temperature—help to make Logan more valuable—and prepare the way for the last upon which I have deliberately thrown out every power of my heart and brain. . . .

It will take some time you know, for the first *novel* of an unknown writer to make its way where it will be read—but let it be read, and I shall not tremble for its fate—nay—I shall not tremble—after a little time—at any *comparison;* but I am impatient—I cannot wait for the gradual accretion of such profit —and therefor I would have you come down upon them (the publick) clap apb clap, before they can get their breath. They are startled at the celebriety of the Scotch novelist—Let us appal them—if we can! . . .

Yours truly
JOHN NEAL

APPENDIX VII

The following letter strikingly exemplifies the well known popularity of Webster's *Grammatical Institute,* first published from 1783 to 1785, and the condition and code of ethics of the publishing trade in 1791.

(To Mathew Carey & Co.)

HARTFORD Aug 14th 1791

Gentlemen

In answer to yours of the 11th current, I give you the state of facts—That under the laws of the U. States, there can be no restriction of the sale of any book *by law.* A man who can *print* the books, recorded under that law, can *sell* them in any part of the U. States. The contrary would be very absurd. But this is no disadvantage to a purchaser of my books, for the right extends to one as well as to another. If you purchase the exclusive right of printing in a certain number of states, your sales are not by *law* confined to those states; & if Mr. Thomas in Massachusetts can send the books to Philadelphia, you can send as many as you please to Mass—. It is therefore agreed by Messrs Hudson & Goodwin & Mess Thomas & Anderson that they will not interfere with each others sales; and I have no doubt they and the proprietors in Vermont would cheerfully sign a writing to that effect. The proprietors have no difference with each other & no clashing. Indeed it is with difficulty that some of them supply the demand at their own stores.

By *"West of the Hudson"* I mean to comprehend all the southern & western states; & it is probable that before the expiration of 13 years, the sale will be considerably extended to the westward of the Allgany. My reason for limiting your sales by the Hudson is this; the City of New York is a large commercial town & traders from great part of New England go there for goods. By this means New York supplies my books for a great extent of territory, & when Mr. Campbells term expires, which will be the May after next, the right returns to me. The right of supplying that city I should not sell for less than 1000 dollars *in hand,* or 150 dollars *annually* for the remaining eleven years. If you were disposed to purchase that right, & either supply the market yourselves or sell to a printer

127

in New York, I do not know that I should have any objections. But the price I set you is *low,* even for the right west of the Hudson; for I find the sales are larger than I apprehended. In short, gentlemen, my intention is that the purchaser in Philadelphia should supply *the whole market* west & south of New Jersey—& also in New Jersey, so far as will suit the commercial interest of the people. Purchasers bordering on the Hudson will get books in New York—those on the Delaware will furnish themselves in Philad. But you will be under no restriction as to sales west of the Hudson. On the other hand, if I should, after Campbells term, supply New York myself, I will bind myself to restrict my sales to that city and the eastward; and the other proprietors are restrained by agreement as well as by the inconvenience of sending books abroad. Neither Hudson & Goodwin nor Thomas & Andrews have, I believe, ever sent a book westward of the Hudson, & yet they are restrained only by their honor & convenience.

I would further inform you th *all* the proprietors have agreed, & a clause is inserted in *every* contract except that of Hudson & Goodwin, which was made long before the United States law was passed, binding them to adhere to some uniform prices in the sales of the books, whenever three fourths of the proprietors shall agree upon the prices—at least that they will not sell below the price agreed upon.

There has been a controversy between Mr. Young, Mr. Campbell Mr Patten & Messrs Hudson & Goodwin; & much injury has accrued to them all—But it has subsided, & the measures I am now taking will prevent the possibility of the like in future. This is my motive for a change in proprietors. All the present proprietors except Mr. Campbell, whose right will soon end, are men who will not injure the business by underselling one another. If you should purchase there will be seven proprietors; so situated as to furnish every part of the U. States without interfering with each other & all men of reputation & honor. And if it should be the wish of any one to form a mutual agreement by writing, both as to the extent of their sales respectively & the prices, I think I can answer for the whole, that such an agreement will be readily formed.

I could wish for your determination soon, as I am informed that one part of the *Institute* is out of print in Philad & an impression wanted.

I am, Gentlemen, with esteem
Your obedi hum Servant,
NOAH WEBSTER JUN.

APPENDIX VIII

The intense competition for first copies of British novels is clearly shown in the two following letters. Primarily however they are here quoted to show what seem to have been the doubtful business methods of the Edinburgh firm, as intimated in the text at page 87.

(To M. Carey & Sons)
  Recd. Nov. 10, (1822)
Gentlemen,
  Since I last wrote to you I have concluded a bargain with Messrs Constable & Co. for *Peveril of the Peak*—one copy of the first volume of which, comes with this by the ship *"Robert Edwards"* the *second* volume will shortly follow, & fragments of the *third* as it is printed. I shall send another copy of volume 1 by the *New York*, which leaves Liverpool on the 1st Octr.— putting it under the especial care of my friend Mr. Isaac Judly —a third, copy of volume 1st will be sent by some other ship & I shall let you have three copies of each of the volumes by different ships. I have engaged to pay twenty five pounds per volume—in all £75.—Nothing has yet reached me from Gibraltar, & judging from the tardiness of your correspondent there, it may probably be delayed for some months. I could not make a better bargain with Constable & Co.—they would not give way in the slightest degree—they have engaged to let me have the last sheets, at least 14 days before they publish in Edinburgh, which will secure you from all danger of disappointment. . . . (He speaks of the "Atlas" which is coming.)
                                                              JOHN MILLER
Fleet Street
  Sept. 24– 1822.

(From M. Carey & Sons)
  MR. JOHN MILLER   Jan. 31st (1823).
  Your favours of 20th & 30th Novr. arrived yesterday with part of Peveril Vol. 3. The first of Vol 2 arrived a short time since per James Monroe but duplicate and trip: have not yet come nor have any of the Copies of Lord Byrons Tragedy arrived. . . .
  We think the demands of Messrs. Constables as improper

as any we have known. They engaged to furnish the book at £75 and it is a matter of no importance to us whether it is in 3 or 4 Vols. These books have always been pubd. in 2 Vols. here at $1.75 or $2 and those of 4 Vols. are always less profitable than those in 3, as they cannot be raised in proportion to the additional matter. We hope, however, you have made some arrangements with them; as it wd be in the highest degree vexatious to us to be delayed. The whole is printed as far as recd—except that which came yesterday, and can have it out in 24 hours from the time the last part is recd. Still if a complete copy arrived in N. York with ours, they could print it in the time it requires our copy to come here and go back. We shd be glad to have all those books in future, but wd wish to have them at as moderate price as possible. for the only advantage we derive from the purchase is the sale of 3 or 4 days until another Edit. can be printed in New York, Boston and here.

This takes place in about 3 days from the time of publishing our Edition or the receipt of an English copy shd that take place before the publication of our's as has several times happened. All the advantage consists in having the whole copy a few days before others, in order that we may send our Edition off in every direction and receive the first sales. They ought to be able to give it 20 or 30 days before publication as *proofs* of the last 3 or 4 half sheets wd answer as well as the best impressions and should there be errors we will take our chances for correcting them ourselves as we have repeatedly done with the former Books. The time required for correction, press work, etc etc, must be very considerable for so large an Edit: and they have afterwards to send it to London so that 20 or 30 days must certainly elapse after they could give proofs of the last form before publication. The conduct of Messrs Constables appears to us very extraordinary. They wrote us[1] saying that the first copies of the Waverley Novels had been stolen from their office and charging us with having employed a person for the purpose, offering at the same time to sell us the copies in the future. We shewed the letters to Mr. Wardle, who had recd them from Hurst Robinson & Co. and sold them to us. He went to London and obtained from Messrs Constable & Co. a certificate that the sheets had been

[1] I have been unable to find the letter from Constable and Company referred to by Carey. Do these letters, revealing as they do the business methods of the Edinburgh firm, throw any light upon the Scott-Constable controversy? A review of the insufficent literature on the subject now at hand leads to no definite conclusion.

furnished by their direction. There appears no little discrepancy between their statements at different times and we think it very shabby of them now to demand an additional sum for Vol. 4 after an express agreement for a *Copy* of the work. At all events we hope you will not fail to get the vol in due time and let us have it. We do not believe there will be any competition for it at £75, as we feel satisfied no other person wd give so much for it for so short a time as we can have the market to ourselves. Let us know as early as you can what will be the next work and secure it on the best terms you can.

Longman & Company have not sent Moores poem[2] to Mr. Wardle. They act curiously with regard to it we hope a copy will arrive to us in good time as it is not worth publishing if any other person receives a copy. Capt. Brenton's Letter has not arrived but from what you say we do not think the work wd answer. We have seen enough of the Prejudice and Nationality of your Countrymen in James's[3] Books and in the retailing of his stories in the Quarterly. As soon as we receive his letters we will answer fully.

[2] Thomas Moore's *Loves of the Angels* is probably the poem referred to.

[3] This was, in all probability, William James, a writer on naval history, who died in 1827. From 1812 to 1813, he was a prisoner of war in the United States. In 1816, he published *An Inquiry into the Merits of the Principal Naval Actions between Great Britain and the United States,* in which his theme was that the naval victories of the Americans were due alone to superiority of numbers. This pamphlet aroused strong feeling in America, as evinced, for instance, in a mild form, here in this letter. The most important work of James was *The Naval History of Great Britain, from the Declaration of War by France in 1793 to the Accession of George IV,* which was issued in five volumes from 1822 to 1824. It appears that an attempt to have it published in the United States drew forth the above remarks.

APPENDIX IX

Some slight idea of the interest of Dickens in things American as well as his change of attitude towards American publishers is given in the following letters.

48 DOUGHTY STREET, LONDON
18th July 1838

Gentlemen

I take the opportunity of my friend, Mr. Thompson, leaving England on a voyage of discovery to the New World, to thank you most cordially for your box of books, and also for your acknowledgment of the popularity of the Pickwick Papers in America, which (both the acknowledgment and the popularity, and especially the last) affords me the greatest delight and satisfaction.

I have never seen your agent, Mr. Miller upon the subject of Nicholas Nickleby, but if I had I should have been unable to have sent you early proofs of any number that has yet appeared as I have been rather behind hand than in advance and have only completed each number a day or two before its publication.

I shall be glad to hear that Nicholas is in favor with our American friends (whom I long to see) and if you can point out to me any means by which, either in this case or in any other, I can give you a preference or serve your interests, believe me that I shall be most willing and prompt to do so.

I am
Gentlemen
Faithfully yours
CHARLES DICKENS

Mess. Carey, Lea & Blanchard

1 DEVONSHIRE TERRACE
YORK GATE, REGENTS PARK,
Tuesday, November Twenty third, 1841.

Dear Sirs:

I have had the pleasure of receiving your welcome letter of the Thirtieth of last month and thank you cordially for its obliging tenor.

I shall be only six months in America altogether; and my present purpose is to land at Boston; go from thence to New

York and thence into the South. Of course I shall visit Philadelphia at some time or other in the half year; and when I do, I shall not fail to see you immediately. It is scarcely possible until one is on your side of the Atlantic to be at all certain as to dates and seasons but as soon as I arrive and have shaped my course minutely, I will write to you again.

In the meanwhile, accept my thanks for your polite attention and the assurance that I am

Dear Sirs
Faithfully yours
CHARLES DICKENS

Mess. Lea & Blanchard

CARLTON HOUSE, NEW YORK.
Thirteenth February, 1842.

My Dear Sirs:

I am cordially obliged to you for your thoughtful recollection and for the box of books. Accept my very best thanks.

I shall be exceedingly glad to know you and shake hands with you when I come to Philadelphia, where I shall be, I hope (though for a very few days) in a fortnight at furthest.

I shall be glad to have too—of course between ourselves—some information on a business point which occurs to my mind just now.

The intelligence of the long faces had reached my ears before I received your letter. I am truly sorry for the cause of their elongation and wish them short again with all my heart.

Dear Sirs
Always Faithfully yours
CHARLES DICKENS

Mess. Lea & Blanchard

NIAGARA FALLS.
Thirteenth April 1842

My Dear Sirs:

Availing myself of your kind offers of service, I am going to trouble you with a few troublesome commissions. If you will execute them for me between this time and the end of May and will send me to New York at the same time a note of the amount you have expended for me in so doing, you will very much oblige me.

1st. Can you get me a good copy of a Book called "History of the Indian Tribes of North America, with biographical Sketches and Anecdotes of the Principal chiefs etc. 120 Portraits. By Thomas L. McKenney and James Hall. Published in Philadelphia by C. Biddle? If it is not very expensive and easily obtained, I should like two copies.

2nd. Will you send me one complete set of my books?

3rdly. Did you republish an English Book called "Lives of the Statesmen of the Commonwealth." By John Forster of the Middle Temple, London? If so, will you send me a copy?

4thly. Will you send me any and every edition of Mr. Talfourd's Tragedy of "Ion" that you can possibly lay your hands on?

There—that's modest. I have quite done.

Faithfully yours always
CHARLES DICKENS

Mess. Lea & Blanchard

CARLTON HOUSE, NEW YORK.
Second of June, 1842.

My Dear Sirs:

I thank you very sincerely for your kind letter and your handsome Present of Books. I shall carry them all home and put them beside your other contributions to my shelves.

My inclination would lead me with a silken cord to Philadelphia. But I am weary of travelling, and am going to lie in the shade of some Trees on the bank of the North river until Tuesday comes—that bright day in my calendar when I turn toward Home and England.

Good bye.

Always believe me
Faithfully your friend,
CHARLES DICKENS

Messrs. Lea & Blanchard

1 DEVONSHIRE TERRACE, YORK GATE, REGENTS PARK
Twenty eighth December 1842.

Dear Sirs:

Rest assured that if any personal or private feeling were intermixed with the resolution at which I arrived when I came home in reference to American republications of my books, it would have great weight in your favor. I formed it on principle. Disgusted with the infamous state of the Law in respect of copyright, and confirmed in the opinion I have always held that there is no reasonable ray of hope of its being changed for many years to come, I determined that so far as I was concerned the American people should have the full pride, honor, glory and profit of it; that I would be no party to its invasion; and that I would have nothing blown to me by a side wind, which the dishonest breath of the popular legislature with-held.

I hope that the more you see of this plunder and the dirty hands into which it goes, the more you will feel and advocate the necessity of a change.

Always believe me
Faithfully yours
CHARLES DICKENS

Mess. Lea & Blanchard

BIBLIOGRAPHY

A fairly complete bibliography of Mathew Carey can be found in J. Sabin's *Bibliotheca Americana*. The works listed below have been of service, but by far the most valuable material in the production of this monograph was the business documents of Mathew Carey and of the publishing firms which succeeded him. These records are not accessible to the public; and no bibliography of them could be formed if they were. It seems unnecessary to refer to the most obvious works of reference on American literature, such as *The National Cyclopedia of American Biography, Appleton's Cyclopedia, Lamb's Biographical Dictionary,* etc., etc.

American Book Circular. Ed. and published by Wiley & Putnam, New York, April, 1843.

American Bookseller. Vol. XVII, No. 3. New York, Feb. 1, 1885.

Appleton, William H., *Letters on International Copyright.* New York, 1872. (Pamphlet, pp. 24.)

Baird, Henry Carey, *Copyright, National and International, An Address.* Philadelphia, 1884. (Pamphlet, pp. 7.)

Bowker, R. R., *Copyright, Its Law and Its Literature. With a Bibliography of Literary Property.* By Thorvald Solberg. New York, 1886.

Bryant, William Cullen, *Address to the People of the United States in behalf of the American Copyright Club, Adopted at New York, October 18, 1843.* New York, 1843. This pamphlet of eighteen pages is signed by Francis L. Hawks and Cornelius Matthews also.

Bryant, William Cullen, *Poetical Works.* New York, 1908.

Carey, Mathew, *Autobiographical Sketches, in a Series of Letters Addressed to a Friend.* Philadelphia, 1829. (A Reprint of this is listed again under *New England Magazine.*)

Carey, Mathew, *The Crisis, An Appeal to the good sense of the nation, against the spirit of resistance and dissolution of the Union.* Philadelphia, 1832.

Carey, Mathew, *Essays on Political Economy; Or the Most Certain Means of Promoting the Wealth, Power, Resources, and Happiness of Nations.* Philadelphia, 1822.

Carey, Mathew, *Letters on Religious Persecution, Proving that the most Heinous of Crimes, has not been peculiar to Roman Catholics.* Fourth Edition, Philadelphia, 1829.

Carey, Mathew. *Miscellaneous Essays.* Philadelphia, 1830.

Carey, Mathew, *The New Olive Branch: Or, An Attempt to Establish an Identity of Interest between Agriculture, Manufactures, and Commerce.* Philadelphia, 1820.

Carey, Mathew, *The Olive Branch: Or, Faults on both Sides, Federal and Democratic. A Serious Appeal to the Necessity of Mutual Forgiveness and Harmony.* Sixth Edition, Philadelphia, 1815.

Carey, Mathew, *Vindiciae Hibernicae: Or Ireland Vindicated.* Philadelphia, 1819.

Congressional Record. Vol. XIX. Washington, 1888.

Derby, J. C., *Fifty Years among Authors, Books and Publishers.* New York, 1884.

Drone, Eaton S., *A Treatise on the Law of Property in Intellectual Productions in Great Britain and the United States.* Boston, 1879.

Dunlap, William, *A History of the American Theater.* New York, 1832.

Ford, Paul Lester, *The Writings of Thomas Jefferson.* New York & London, 1899.

Garnett, Richard, " Early Spanish-American Printing," in *The Library,* Vol. I., London, 1900.

Goddard, Harold Clarke, *Studies in New England Transcendentalism.* New York, 1908.

Green, Samuel A., *Ten fac-simile reproductions relating to New England.* Boston, 1902.

Growoll, A., *Book-Trade Bibliography in the United States in the XIX Century.* New York, 1898.

Harrison, James A., *The Complete Works of Edgar Allan Poe.* New York, 1902.

Hildeburn, Charles R., *Issues of the Press in Pennsylvania, 1685-1784.* Philadelphia, 1887.

Houghton, Henry O., *Early Printing in America.* Montpelier, 1894.

Jackson, M. Katherine, *Outlines of the Literary History of Colonial Pennsylvania.* Lancaster, 1906.

L'Estrange, Rev. A. G. K., *The Life of Mary Russel Mitford.* New York, 1870.

Loliée, Frederic. *A Short History of Comparative Literature.* London, 1906.

Loshe, Lillie Deming, *The Early American Novel.* New York, 1907.

Lounsbury, Thomas R., *James Fenimore Cooper.* Boston, 1883.

McMaster, John Bach. *A History of the People of the United States.* New York, 1900.

New England Magazine, The. Volumes 5, 6, and 7. Boston, 1833-4.

North American Review, The. Volume 55. New York, 1842.

Oberholzer, Ellis Paxton, *The Literary History of Philadelphia.* Philadelphia, 1906.

Oliver, Grace A., *A Study of Maria Edgeworth.* Boston, 1882.

Port Folio, The. Volume 7. Philadelphia, 1811.

Putnam, George Haven, *The Question of the Copyright.* New York, 1891. (This is a series of articles by R. R. Bowker, Brander Matthews, G. H. Putnam, W. E. Simonds, Sir James Stephen, and Walter Besant, with extracts from speeches delivered in the Senate in 1891, etc., compiled by George Haven Putnam. Reference might also be made to *A Memoir of George Palmer Putnam Together with a Record of the Publishing House founded by Him.* By George Haven Putnam. Two volumes. New York, 1903. This work is, however, of no particular value for our immediate purpose.

Rivington, Charles Robert, "Notes on the Stationers' Company," in *The Library.* Vol. IV. London, 1903.

Scudder, Horace E., *Noah Webster,* Boston, 1882.

Senate Reports. Vol. 7. Washington, 1886.

Smith, R. Pearsall, *Anglo-American Copyright,* Extracted from *The Nineteenth Century,* No. 129, November, 1887. This is a reprint in pamphlet form, with comments by Gladstone, Lord Tennyson, Rider Haggard, Justin McCarthy, Walter Besant, Matthew Arnold, Huxley and others.

Smyth, A. H., *The Philadelphia Magazines and their Contributors.* Philadelphia, 1892.

Southern Literary Messenger, The. Ed. by Edgar Allan Poe. Vol. II., Richmond, 1836.

INDEX

VITA

The author of this dissertation received his secondary training in the First Missouri Normal, Kirksville, Missouri. In 1899 he entered the freshman class of William Jewell College, Liberty, Missouri. He entered the University of Missouri in 1900, and took courses in literature under Professors E. A. Allen, H. C. Penn, H. M. Belden, Raymond Weeks, and others, receiving the degree of B.A. in 1903. He was enrolled in the graduate school of Columbia University, in the Department of English, from 1903 to 1906, and during that time took courses in Comparative Literature under Professor J. E. Spingarn, and in English Literature under Professors W. P. Trent, Brander Matthews, G. R. Carpenter, W. A. Neilson (now of Harvard University), F. T. Baker, G. P. Krapp, W. W. Lawrence, and Dr. C. M. Hathaway. He received the degree of A.M. in 1904. In 1906–7 he was Instructor in English in the University of Missouri. He took work under Professor Henry Sweet and others at Oxford University in 1907. During 1907–8 he was a student at the University of Berlin. Here he worked under Professors Alois Brandl, W. H. Schofield (Exchange Professor from Harvard University), Dr. Delmer, and others. During the Summer School of Columbia University for 1910, he was a student under Professor Harry Ayers. He was Instructor in English at the University of Illinois from 1908 to 1911. In 1911 he was appointed to a position at Dartmouth College.